ON THE
JOB
SERIES

REAL PEOPLE
WORKING *in*

GOVERNMENT

ON THE JOB SERIES

REAL PEOPLE WORKING *in*

GOVERNMENT

Blythe Camenson

VGM Career Horizons
NTC/Contemporary Publishing Group

Library of Congress Cataloging-in-Publication Data

Camenson, Blythe.
    Real people working in government / Blythe Camenson.
        p.   cm.—(On the job series)
    ISBN 0-8442-4710-3.—ISBN 0-8442-4711-1 (pbk.)
    1. Civil service positions—United States.   2. Municipal
government—Vocational guidance—United States.   3. Local
government—Vocational guidance—United States.   I. Title.
II. Series.
    JK16.C32   1998
    351.73′023—dc21   97-35169
                                                CIP

Published by VGM Career Horizons
A division of NTC/Contemporary Publishing Group, Inc.
4255 West Touhy Avenue, Lincolnwood (Chicago), Illinois 60646-1975 U.S.A.
Printed in the United States of America
International Standard Book Number: 0-8442-4710-3 (cloth)
                                      0-8442-4711-1 (paper)
15   14   13   12   11   10   9   8   7   6   5   4   3   2   1

Contents

Acknowledgments

The author would like to thank the following professionals for providing information about their careers:

- Brian Adams, Electronic Systems Engineer

- Barbara Arrants, Public Defender

- Jane E. Bennett, Vocational Rehabilitation Counselor

- Rob Brantley, Extrication Specialist

- Diane B. Camerlo, In-House Counsel, Federal Reserve Bank

- Nick Delia, Letter Carrier

- Dawn Edwards, IRS Agent

- Rick Fitzgerald, Deputy Sheriff

- Samantha Kievman, Firefighter

- James Lanuti, Circuit Judge

- Robert Manzanares, Administrative Officer

- Jonas Martin Frost, U.S. Congressman

- Jerry O'Brien, Driver/Engineer

- Elsa Riehl, Post Office Window Clerk

- Timothy Sikora, Aerospace Engineer

- Joseph Tringali, Assistant State Attorney General

- Jim Van Laningham, General Services Officer

- John Wiorek, Law Clerk

How to Use This Book

On the Job: Real People Working in Government is part of a series of career books designed to help you find essential information quickly and easily. Unlike other career resources on the market, books in the *On the Job* series provide you with information on hundreds of careers, in an easy-to-use format. This includes information on

- The nature of the work
- Working conditions
- Employment
- Training, other qualifications, and advancement
- Job outlooks
- Earnings
- Related occupations
- Sources of additional information

But that's not all. You'll also benefit from a firsthand look at what the jobs are really like, as told in the words of the employees themselves. Throughout the book, one-on-one interviews with dozens of practicing professionals enrich the text and enhance your understanding of life on the job.

These interviews tell what each job entails, what the duties are, what the lifestyle is like, what the upsides and downsides are. All of the professionals reveal what drew them to the field and how they got started. And, to help you make the best career choice for yourself, each professional offers you some expert advice based on years of experience.

Each chapter also lets you see at a glance, with easy-to-reference symbols, the level of education required and salary range for the featured occupations.

So, how do you use this book? Easy. You don't need to run to the library and bury yourself in cumbersome documents from the Bureau of Labor Statistics, nor do you need to rush out and buy a lot of bulky books you'll never plow through. All you have to do is glance through our extensive table of contents, find the fields that interest you, and read what the experts have to say.

Introduction to the Field

People who work in government careers give of themselves in many different capacities, providing a valuable service. If you're reading this book, chances are you're already considering a career in one of the many areas of this wide-open occupational category. Glancing through the table of contents will give you an idea of all the choices open to you.

But perhaps you're not sure of the working conditions the different fields offer or about which area would suit your personality, skills, and lifestyle the most. There are several factors to consider when deciding which sector to pursue. Each field carries with it different levels of responsibility and commitment. To identify occupations that will match your expectations, you need to know what each job entails.

Ask yourself the following questions and make note of your answers. Then, as you go through the following chapters, compare your requirements to the information provided by the professionals interviewed. Their comments will help you pinpoint the fields that would interest you and eliminate those that would clearly be the wrong choice.

- How much time are you willing to commit to training? Some skills can be learned on-the-job or in a year or two of formal training; others can take considerably longer.

- Do you want to work in an office behind a desk or would you prefer to be out and about, meeting with the public or clients in their homes—or prison?

- Can you handle a certain amount of stress on the job, or would you prefer a quiet—and safe—environment?

- How much money do you expect to earn starting out and after you have a few years' experience under your belt? Salaries and earnings vary greatly in each chosen profession.

- How much independence do you require? If you'd prefer to be your own boss, then maybe a career in government work would not be the right choice for you.

- Would you rather work daytime hours, or would you prefer evenings or weekends?

- Can you pay attention to detail and handle paperwork, legal documents, and reports?

Knowing what your expectations are and comparing them to the realities of the work will help you make informed choices.

Although *On the Job: Real People Working in Government* strives to be as comprehensive as possible, it does not cover all jobs in this extensive field or give them the same amount of emphasis. You will find information on other related professions in the following *On the Job* books published by VGM Career Horizons:

On the Job: Real People Working in Service Businesses

On the Job: Real People Working in the Helping Professions

On the Job: Real People Working in Law

On the Job: Real People Working in Engineering

If you still have questions after reading this book, there are a number of other avenues to pursue. You can find out more information by contacting the sources listed at the end of each chapter. You can also find professionals on your own to talk to and observe as they go about their work. Any remaining gaps you discover can be filled by referring to the *Occupational Outlook Handbook.*

CHAPTER 1

Chief Executives and Legislators

🎓 EDUCATION
B.A. required; master's
preferred

$$$ SALARY
$12,000–$200,000

OVERVIEW

Go to school. Pay your taxes. Register for the draft. Stop at the stop sign. It seems as though the government is always telling us what to do. Who tells the government what to do? Chief executives and legislators at the federal, state, and local level do the telling. They are elected or appointed officials who strive to meet the needs of their constituents with an effective and efficient government.

Chief executives are officials who run governmental units that help formulate, carry out, and enforce laws. These officials include the president and vice president of the United States, senators, congressmen and congresswomen, state governors and lieutenant governors, county executives, town and township officials, mayors, and city, county, town, and township managers. All are elected except for local government managers, who are appointed by the local government council or commission.

Government chief executives, like corporation presidents and other chief executives, have overall responsibility for how their organizations perform. In coordination with legislators, they establish goals and objectives and then organize programs and form policies to attain these goals. They appoint people to head departments, such as highway, health, police, park and recreation, economic development, and finance. Through these departmental heads, chief executives oversee the work of civil servants, who carry out programs and enforce laws enacted by the legislative bodies. They prepare budgets, specifying how government resources will be used. They ensure, by holding staff conferences, requiring work schedules and periodic performance reports, and conducting personal inspections, that their government uses resources properly and carries out programs as planned.

Chief executives meet with legislators and constituents to solicit their ideas, discuss programs, and elicit their support. They also may confer with leaders of other governments to solve mutual problems. Chief executives nominate citizens for government boards and commissions to oversee government activities or examine and help the government solve problems such as drug abuse, crime, deteriorating roads, and inadequate public education.

They also solicit bids from and select contractors to do work for the government, encourage business investment and economic development in their jurisdictions, and seek federal or state funds.

Chief executives of large jurisdictions rely on a staff of aides and assistants; those of small ones often do much of the work themselves.

City, county, town, and other managers, although appointed officials, may act as and refer to themselves as chief executives.

Legislators are the elected officials who make laws or amend existing ones in order to remedy problems or to promote certain activities. They include U.S. senators and representatives, state senators and representatives (called *assemblymen* and *assemblywomen*, or *delegates* in some states), county legislators (called *supervisors*, *commissioners*, or *council members*, or *freeholders* in some states), and city and town council members (called *aldermen* and *alderwomen*, *trustees*, *clerks*, *supervisors*, *magistrates*, and *commissioners*, among other titles).

Legislators introduce bills in the legislative body and examine and vote on bills introduced by other legislators. In preparing legislation, they read reports and work with constituents, representatives of interest groups, members of boards and commissions, the chief executive and department heads, consultants, and legislators in other units of government. They also approve budgets and the appointments of department heads and commission members submitted by the chief executive. In some jurisdictions, the legislative body appoints a city, town, or county manager. Many legislators, especially at the state and federal levels, have a staff to help research, prepare legislation, and resolve constituents' problems.

In some units of government, the line between legislative and executive functions blurs. For example, mayors and city managers may draft legislation and conduct council meetings, and council members may oversee the operation of departments.

Working conditions of chief executives and legislators vary depending on the size of the governmental unit. Time spent at work ranges from once-a-month meetings for a local council member to sixty or more hours per week for a legislator. U.S. senators and representatives, governors and lieutenant governors, and chief executives and legislators in some large local jurisdictions work full-time year-round, as do almost all county and city managers.

Some city and town managers work for several small jurisdictions. Most state legislators work full time while legislatures are in session (usually for a few months a year) and part time the rest of the year. Local elected officials in most jurisdictions work part time; however, even though their jobs are officially designated part-time, some incumbents actually work a full-time schedule.

In addition to their regular schedules, chief executives are on call at all hours to handle emergencies.

Some jobs require only occasional out-of-town travel, but others involve more frequent travel to attend sessions of the legislature or to meet with officials of other units of government. Officials in districts covering a large area may drive long distances to perform their regular duties.

TRAINING

Choosing from among candidates who meet the minimum age, residency, and citizenship requirements, the voters try to elect the individual they decide is most fit to hold the position at stake. The question is thus not how does one become qualified, but how does one get elected?

Successful candidates usually have a strong record of accomplishment in paid and unpaid work. Many have business, teaching, or legal experience, but others come from a wide variety of occupations. In addition, many have served as volunteers on school boards or zoning commissions; with charities, political action groups, and political campaigns; or with religious, fraternal, and similar organizations.

Work experience and public service help develop the planning, organizing, negotiating, motivating, fundraising, budgeting, public speaking, and problem-solving skills needed to run a political campaign. Candidates must make decisions quickly and fairly with little or contradictory information. They must have confidence in themselves and their employees to inspire and motivate their constituents and their staffs. They should also be sincere and candid, presenting their views thoughtfully and convincingly.

Additionally, they must know how to hammer out compromises with colleagues and constituents. National and statewide campaigns also require a good deal of energy, stamina, and fundraising skills.

Town, city, and county managers are appointed by a council or commission. Managers come from a variety of educational backgrounds. A master's degree in public administration, including coursework in public financial management and legal issues in public administration, is widely recommended but not required. Virtually all town, city, and county managers have at least a bachelor's degree, and many hold a master's degree. In addition, a student internship in government is recommended; the experience and personal contacts acquired can prove invaluable in securing a position as a town, city, or county manager.

Generally, a town, city, or county manager in a smaller jurisdiction is required to have some expertise in a wide variety of areas; managers who work for larger jurisdictions specialize in financial, administrative, or personnel matters. For all managers, communication skills and the ability to get along with others are essential.

Advancement opportunities for most elected public officials are not clearly defined. Because elected positions normally require a period of residency and because local public support is critical, officials can usually advance to other offices only in the jurisdictions where they live. For example, council members may run for mayor or for a position in the state government, and state legislators may run for governor or for Congress. Many officials are not politically ambitious, however, and do not seek advancement. Others lose their bids for reelection or voluntarily leave the occupation. A lifetime career as a government chief executive or legislator is rare.

Town, city, and county managers have a clearer career path. A manager generally obtains a master's degree in public administration and then gains experience as a management analyst or an assistant in a government department working with councils and chief executives and learning about planning, budgeting, civil engineering, and other aspects of running a city. After several years, he or she may be hired to manage a town or a small city and may eventually become manager of progressively larger cities.

JOB OUTLOOK

About five of six government chief executives and legislators work in local government; the rest work primarily in state governments. The federal government has 535 senators and representatives and two chief executives—the president and vice president.

There are about 7,500 state legislators and, according to the International City/County Management Association (ICMA), about 11,000 city managers. Executives and council members for local governments make up the remainder.

Chief executives and legislators who do not hold full-time, year-round positions normally work in second occupations as well (commonly the ones they held before being elected), are retired from other occupations, or attend to household responsibilities. Business owner or manager, teacher, and lawyer are common second occupations, and there are many others as well.

Little, if any, growth is expected in the number of government chief executives and legislators through the year 2005. Few, if any, new governments are likely to form, and the number of chief executives and legislators in existing governments rarely changes.

The addition of one or two new states to the union would lead to several additional U.S. senators and representatives. Some small increase may occur as growing communities in the rapidly growing south and west, for example, become independent cities and towns and elect chief executives and legislators and, perhaps, appoint town managers.

A few new positions may also develop as cities and counties without managers hire managers and as unpaid offices that are not counted as employment are converted to paid positions.

On the other hand, attempts by governments to cut costs and streamline operations, in response to tight budgets, could reduce the number of paid positions, particularly at the local level.

The number of state legislators recently declined slightly when states, as required by law, completed their decennial redistricting.

Elections give newcomers the chance to unseat incumbents or to fill vacated positions. In many elections, there is substantial competition, although the level of competition varies from jurisdiction to jurisdiction and from year to year. Generally, there is less competition in small jurisdictions that have part-time positions offering relatively low salaries and little or no staff to help with tedious work than there is in large jurisdictions that have full-time positions offering higher salaries, more staff, and greater status.

In some cases, usually in small jurisdictions, an incumbent runs unopposed or an incumbent resigns, leaving only one candidate for a job. The high cost of running for such positions in large jurisdictions may serve as a deterrent to running or may leave the challenger dependent on contributions from special interest groups.

SALARIES

Earnings of public administrators vary widely, depending on the size of the government unit and on whether the job is part time, full time and year-round, or full time for only a few months a year. Salaries range from little or nothing for a small town council member to $200,000 a year for the president of the United States.

According to ICMA, the average annual salary of mayors runs about $10,000. In cities with a population under 2,500, salaries average about $1,800; in cities with a population over one million, salaries average around $78,000.

ICMA data indicate that the average salary is about $70,000 for county managers and $66,000 for city managers. Salaries range from $35,000 in towns with fewer than 2,500 residents to $127,000 in cities with populations over one million.

According to *Book of the States, 1994–95,* published by the Council of State Governments, gubernatorial annual salaries range from $60,000 in Arkansas to $130,000 in New York. In addition to receiving a salary, most governors receive perquisites such as transportation and official residences. Lieutenant governors average over $57,000 annually.

In 1995 U.S. senators and representatives earned $133,600, the Senate and House majority and minority leaders $148,400, and the vice president $171,500.

RELATED FIELDS

Related occupations include managerial positions that require a broad range of skills in addition to administrative expertise, such as corporate chief executive and board member positions and the positions of generals in the military.

INTERVIEW
Jonas Martin Frost
U.S. Congressman (D)

U.S. Congressman Jonas Martin Frost, a Democrat, was elected to Congress in 1978 as a representative from Texas in the Dallas/Fort Worth area. He graduated from the University of Missouri in Columbia *in 1966 with two degrees: a B.A. and a B.Jour. (journalism). He earned his J.D. (juris doctor) degree from Georgetown University in Washington, D.C. in 1972.*

Prior to coming to Congress he was a reporter for the Wilmington, Delaware, daily newspaper and the Congressional Quarterly in Washington, and he practiced law in Dallas.

He began his service in the U.S. House of Representatives in January of 1979 and has served continuously since that date.

What the Job Is Really Like

"My responsibilities now are to vote on issues that are important to my district and the nation as a whole. I represent over 566,000 people in the U.S. Congress, and while it is difficult to represent all of them on the same issues, I must try to bring as many pertinent facts together to make a decision on issues in the best interest of these groups.

"My typical day begins around 6:00 A.M. and generally goes until about 10:00 P.M. each evening. The simple things that are associated with the position are the receptions, constituent meetings—where I inform them as to what has happened in Congress—and the other ceremonies that are attached to the position, such as swearing-in ceremonies for new citizens or constituents who are named to positions of trust [public offices] and dedications of new businesses in the district.

"The difficult part of the day is spending endless hours in committee meetings, where you gain information on bills and resolutions that may affect millions of people in the nation—bills such as mandating young men to register for the draft; determining the amount of income tax that will be taken from all Americans; the Pure Water Act, which protects the drinking water of the nation; the Environmental Protection Act, which dictates how to clean up toxic waste sites in America; international trade legislation, such as NAFTA, which regulates the amount of trade that may be tax-free from Mexico and other nations.

"The job can be very tiring, especially the many trips on airplanes that are required to return to my congressional district to make personal appearances to report on the activities of

Congress and to meet with constituents about problems they are having—in an effort to help them if I can. There are always a variety of problems: sons or daughters wanting to get into military academies; companies unilaterally trying to eliminate health insurance programs for their retired employees; obtaining emergency loans for farmers who lose crops because of drought or flood—that sort of thing.

"The work atmosphere is enjoyable. The Congress of the United States is generally composed of hard-working men and women who spend many hours in their efforts to make the United States a better nation. Washington, D.C., is our historic capital, and it is always a thrill and honor to be able to work here as I do.

"I like having the opportunity to have direct input into the decision-making function for our government. I represent more than 566,000 people on every issue that I vote on, and few people ever have that chance."

How Congressman Frost Got Started

"During the time of my employment by *Congressional Quarterly*, where I covered the events in Congress, I became convinced that I could be a good representative, serving the interests of my home district in Dallas, Texas. The experience at *CQ* gave me the insight and contacts within the House of Representatives to achieve a good start once I was elected in 1978.

"My first job was as a staff person on the old *Fort Worth Press*, which is no longer in existence. That gave me the experience to move to a daily newspaper and to later join a television panel in Dallas where I reported on legal matters within the community. The program was called *Newsroom*, and its anchor was Jim Lehrer during the time he was in Dallas.

"I decided to run for Congress and I knew it was important to pick a district in which I'd feel comfortable . . . with how you think the district feels on issues and with the customs of the area. The Dallas–Fort Worth area was good for me, as I was born in Fort Worth, Texas, and was familiar with the Dallas–Fort Worth area.

"I went about talking to various known community leaders, political activists, and media representatives . . . all of whom would know the political atmosphere of the community.

I was running against an incumbent congressman and there is always a group that opposes an incumbent, so it was a bit easier to create a political organization on that basis, rather than running in a district in which no incumbent was running.

"I chose the Democratic Party because I believe the general philosophy of the party is closer to my own . . . feelings on how people should be treated by the government, what role the government plays in daily lives, the extent to which government should develop, etc. This is a very personal consideration that comes after years of watching the direction in which a particular party will lead the nation when that party is in power.

"I chose to run for the House rather than the Senate for several reasons:

1. Familiarity with the total area in which I would be running, rather than having to run statewide in Texas. . . . That's a large area.

2. Finances. I was able to raise enough money to conduct a good campaign on the local level. The cost of running statewide would not have been within my reach at the time of my election to the House.

3. I was familiar with the rules and operations of the House from my days as a reporter for the *Congressional Quarterly*, where I covered the proceedings of the House.

"I lost the first election in 1974. I was very disappointed but never had the slightest doubt that I would run again. I had received 46 percent of the vote in 1974, so it seemed that the goal was obtainable. After my loss in 1974, I practiced law until winning the election four years later, in 1978.

"There are no term limits for serving in the U.S. House of Representatives. I am currently in my ninth two-year term. (The House has two-year terms, with all members' terms ending after two years. The Senate has six-year terms.)

"I have no plans to leave congressional service. If I were to retire or leave the service of the Congress for any reason, I would likely return to the practice of law in Dallas."

Expert Advice

"If you have a desire to serve in public office, you should be absolutely sure of your willingness to serve long hours and be willing to take a lot of criticism for your decisions—because you cannot represent everyone's position on every issue.

"If you make the decision that you want to seek public office, then do so. It is a meaningful experience in just seeking the office, whether you win or lose. I lost the first race I made for Congress. Four years later, I still had the dream of serving in the Congress. I ran again and won."

●   ●   ●

FOR MORE INFORMATION

For more information on careers in public administration, consult your elected representatives and local library.

Information on state governments can be obtained from

> Council of State Governments
> P.O. Box 11910
> Iron Works Pike
> Lexington, KY 40578

Information on appointed officials in local government can be obtained from

> International City/County Management Association
> 777 North Capitol Street NE, Suite 500
> Washington, DC 20002

CHAPTER 2 The Legal System

EDUCATION
law school

$$$ SALARY
$25,000–$80,000

OVERVIEW
Attorneys

Attorneys, also called *lawyers*, act as both advocates and advisors in our society. As advocates, they represent one of the opposing parties in criminal and civil trials by presenting in court evidence that supports their clients. As advisors, lawyers counsel their clients about their legal rights and obligations and suggest particular courses of action in business and personal matters. Whether acting as advocates or advisors, all attorneys interpret the law and apply it to specific situations. This requires research and communication abilities.

Lawyers perform in-depth research into the purposes behind the applicable laws and into judicial decisions that have been applied to those laws under circumstances similar to those currently faced by their clients.

While all lawyers continue to make use of law libraries to prepare cases, some supplement their search of the conventional printed sources with computer software packages that automatically search the legal literature and identify legal texts that may be relevant to a specific subject. In litigation that involves many supporting documents, lawyers may also use computers to organize and index the material.

Tax lawyers also use computers to make tax computations and explore alternative tax strategies for clients.

Lawyers then communicate to others the information obtained from research. They advise what actions clients may take and draw up legal documents, such as wills and contracts, for clients.

Lawyers must deal with people in a courteous, efficient manner and not disclose matters discussed in confidence with clients. They hold positions of great responsibility and are obligated to adhere to strict rules of ethics.

SPECIALIZATIONS

Trial Lawyers. The more detailed aspects of a lawyer's job depend upon his or her field of specialization and position. Even though all lawyers are allowed to represent parties in court, some appear in court more frequently than others. Lawyers who specialize in trial work need an exceptional ability to think quickly and speak with ease and authority and must be thoroughly familiar with courtroom rules and strategy. Even trial lawyers spend most of their time outside the courtroom, conducting research, interviewing clients and witnesses, and handling other details in preparation for trial.

Besides specializing in trials, lawyers may specialize in other areas. The majority of lawyers are in private practice where they may concentrate on criminal or civil law.

Government Attorneys. Attorneys employed at the various levels of government make up a large category. Lawyers that work for state attorneys general, prosecutors, public defenders, and courts play a key role in the criminal justice system. At the federal level, attorneys investigate cases for the Department of Justice or other agencies. Also, lawyers at every government level help develop programs, draft laws, interpret legislation, establish enforcement procedures, and argue civil and criminal cases on behalf of the government.

Law Clerks. Law clerks are fully trained attorneys who choose to work with judges, either for one- to two-year stints out of law school or as full-time, professional careers. Their duties involve mainly research and writing reports.

Criminal Lawyers. Criminal lawyers represent persons who have been charged with crimes, arguing their cases in courts of law.

Civil Lawyers. Civil attorneys assist clients with litigation, wills, trusts, contracts, mortgages, titles, and leases. Trustees manage people's property, and executors see that provisions of clients' wills are carried out. Other civil lawyers handle only public interest cases, civil or criminal, that have potential impacts extending well beyond the individual clients.

Other lawyers work for legal aid societies, which are private, nonprofit organizations established to serve disadvantaged people. These lawyers generally handle civil rather than criminal cases.

Some other specializations within civil law include

- bankruptcy

- probate

- international law

- environmental law

- intellectual property

- insurance law

- family law

- real estate law

- public defender

House Counsel. Lawyers sometimes are employed full time by a single client. If the client is a corporation, the lawyer is known as a *house counsel* and usually advises the company about legal questions that arise from its business activities. These questions might involve patents, government regulations, contracts with other companies, property interests, or collective bargaining agreements with unions.

Law Professors. A relatively small number of trained attorneys work in law schools. Most are faculty members who specialize in one or more subjects, but others serve as administrators. Some work full time in nonacademic settings and teach part time.

Lawyers and judges do most of their work in offices, law libraries, and courtrooms. Lawyers sometimes meet in clients' homes or places of business and, when necessary, in hospitals or prisons. They frequently travel to attend meetings; to gather evidence; and to appear before courts, legislative bodies, and other authorities.

Salaried lawyers in government and private corporations generally have structured work schedules. Lawyers in private practice may work irregular hours while conducting research, conferring with clients, or preparing briefs during nonoffice hours.

Lawyers often work long hours, and about half regularly work fifty hours or more per week. They are under particularly heavy pressure when their cases are being tried. Preparation for court includes keeping abreast of the latest laws and judicial decisions.

Although the work of lawyers generally is not seasonal, the work of tax lawyers and other specialists may be an exception. Because lawyers in private practice may often determine their own workload and when they will retire, many stay in practice well beyond the usual retirement age.

EDUCATION
law school

$$$ SALARY
$64,000–$171,500

Judges

Judges apply the law. They oversee the legal process that in courts of law resolves civil disputes and determines guilt in criminal cases according to federal and state laws and those of local jurisdictions.

They preside over cases touching on virtually every aspect of society, from traffic offenses to disputes over management of professional sports and from the rights of huge corporations to questions concerning disconnecting life support equipment for terminally ill persons. They must ensure that trials and hearings are conducted fairly and that the court administers justice in a manner that safeguards the legal rights of all parties involved.

Judges preside over trials or hearings and listen as attorneys representing the parties involved present and argue their cases. They rule on the admissibility of evidence and methods of conducting testimony, and they settle disputes between the opposing attorneys. They ensure that rules and procedures are followed, and if unusual circumstances arise for which standard procedures have not been established, judges direct how trials will proceed based on their knowledge of the law.

Judges often hold pretrial hearings for cases. They listen to allegations and, based on the evidence presented, determine whether there is enough merit in the evidence for a trial to be held. In criminal cases, judges may decide that persons charged with crimes should be held in jail pending their trials or may set conditions for release through the trials. In civil cases, judges may impose restrictions upon the parties until trials are held.

When trials are held, juries are often selected to decide cases. However, judges decide cases when the law does not require a jury trial or when the parties waive their right to a jury. Judges instruct juries on applicable laws, direct them to deduce the facts from the evidence presented, and hear their verdict.

In many states, judges sentence those convicted in criminal cases. They also award relief to litigants, including, where appropriate, compensation for damages in civil cases.

Judges also work outside the courtroom in chambers. In their private offices, judges read documents on pleadings and motions, research legal issues, hold hearings with lawyers, write opinions, and oversee court operations. Running a court is like running a small business, and judges manage their courts' administrative and clerical staff, too.

Judges' duties vary according to the extent of their jurisdictions and powers. General trial court judges of the federal and state court systems have jurisdiction over any cases in their systems. They generally try civil cases that transcend the jurisdiction of lower courts and all cases involving felony offenses.

Federal and state appellate court judges, although few in number, have the power to overrule decisions made by trial court or administrative law judges if they determine that legal errors were made or if legal precedent does not support the judgments of lower courts. They rule on fewer cases than do general trial court judges and rarely have direct contact with the people involved.

The majority of state court judges preside in courts in which jurisdiction is limited by law to certain types of cases. A variety of titles are assigned to these judges, but among the most common are *municipal court judge, county court judge, magistrate*, and *justice of the peace*. Traffic violations, misdemeanors, small claims cases, and pretrial hearings constitute the bulk of the work of these judges, but some states allow them to handle cases involving domestic relations, probate, contracts, and selected other areas of the law.

Administrative law judges, formerly called *hearing officers*, are employed by government agencies to rule on appeals of agency administrative decisions. They make decisions on a person's eligibility for various Social Security benefits or worker's compensation, protection of the environment, enforcement of health and safety regulations, employment discrimination, and compliance with economic regulatory requirements.

Many judges work a standard forty-hour week, but a third of all judges work over fifty hours per week. Some judges with limited jurisdiction are employed part time and divide their time between their judicial responsibilities and other careers.

Judges held 90,000 jobs in 1992. All worked for federal, state, or local governments, with about half holding positions in the federal government. The majority of the remainder were employed at the state level.

TRAINING FOR ATTORNEYS

To practice law in the courts of any state or other jurisdiction, a person must be licensed or admitted to its bar under rules established by the jurisdiction's highest court. Nearly all jurisdictions require that applicants for admission to the bar pass a written bar examination. Most jurisdictions also require applicants to pass a separate written ethics examination. Lawyers who have been admitted to the bar in one jurisdiction occasionally may be admitted to the bar in another without taking an examination if they meet the second jurisdiction's standards of good moral character and have a specified period of legal experience.

Federal courts and agencies set their own qualifications for those practicing before them.

To qualify for the bar examination in most states, an applicant must complete at least three years of college and graduate from a law school approved by the American Bar Association (ABA) or the proper state authorities.

ABA approval signifies that the law school and particularly its library and faculty meet certain standards developed by the ABA to promote quality legal education. In 1992, the ABA approved 177 law schools. Others were approved by state authorities only. With certain exceptions, graduates of schools not approved by the ABA are restricted to taking the bar examination and practicing in the state or other jurisdiction in which the school is located; most of these schools are in California.

Seven states accept the study of law solely in a law office or in combination with study in a law school; only California accepts the study of law by correspondence as qualification for taking the bar examination.

Several states require registration and approval of students by the State Board of Law Examiners, either before they enter law school or during the early years of legal study.

Although there is no nationwide bar examination, forty-six states, the District of Columbia, Guam, the Northern Mariana Islands, and the Virgin Islands require the six-hour Multistate Bar Examination (MBE) as part of the bar examination; the MBE is not required in Indiana, Iowa, Louisiana, Washington, and Puerto Rico. The MBE, covering issues of broad interest, is given in addition to a locally prepared six-hour state bar examination. The three-hour Multistate Essay Examination (MEE) is used as part of the state bar examination in a few states. States vary in their use of MBE and MEE scores.

The required college and law school education usually involves seven years of full-time study after high school including four years of undergraduate study, followed by three years in law school. Although some law schools accept a very small number of students after three years of college, most require applicants to have a bachelor's degree. To meet the needs of students who can attend only part time, a number of law schools have night or part-time divisions that usually require four years of study. In 1991, about one of six students in ABA-approved schools were attending part time.

Preparation for a career as a lawyer really begins in college. Although there is no recommended prelaw major, the choice of an undergraduate program is important. Certain courses and activities are desirable because they give the student the skills needed to succeed both in law school and in the profession.

Essential skills include proficiency in writing, reading, and analyzing; thinking logically; and communicating verbally. These skills are learned during high school and college. An undergraduate program that cultivates these skills while broadening the student's view of the world is desirable. Courses in English, a foreign language, public speaking, government, philosophy, history, economics, mathematics, and computer science, among other subjects, are useful. Whatever the major, students should not specialize too narrowly.

Students interested in a particular aspect of law may find related courses helpful; for example, many law schools with patent law tracks require bachelor's degrees, or at least several courses, in engineering and science. Future tax lawyers should have a strong undergraduate background in accounting.

Acceptance by most law schools depends on the applicant's ability to demonstrate an aptitude for the study of law, usually accomplished through having good undergraduate grades, performing well on the Law School Admission Test (LSAT), having attended a quality undergraduate school, and having prior work experience and sometimes through participating in a personal interview. However, law schools vary in the weight that they place on each of these factors.

All law schools approved by the ABA require that applicants take the LSAT. Nearly all law schools require that applicants have certified transcripts sent to the Law School Data Assembly Service. This service then sends applicants' LSAT scores and their standardized records of college grades to the law schools of their choice. Both this service and the LSAT are administered by the Law School Admission Services.

Competition for admission to many law schools is intense. Enrollments rose very rapidly during the 1970s, with applicants far outnumbering available seats. Since then, law school enrollments have remained relatively unchanged, and the number of applicants has fluctuated. However, the number of applicants to most law schools still greatly exceeds the number that can be admitted. Enrollments are expected to remain at about their present level through the year 2005, and competition for admission to the more prestigious law schools will remain keen.

During the first year or year and a half of law school, students generally study fundamental courses such as constitutional law, contracts, property law, torts, civil procedure, and legal writing. In the remaining time, they may elect specialized courses in fields such as tax, labor, or corporation law. Law students often acquire practical experience by participating in school-sponsored legal aid or legal clinic activities, in their schools' moot court competitions in which students conduct appellate arguments, in practice trials under the supervision of experienced lawyers and judges, and through research and writing on legal issues for their schools' law journals.

In 1994, law students in thirty-eight states were required to pass the Multistate Professional Responsibility Examination (MPRE), which tests their knowledge of the ABA codes on professional responsibility and judicial conduct. In some states, the MPRE may be taken during law school, usually after students complete a course on legal ethics.

A number of law schools have clinical programs in which students gain legal experience through practice trials and law school projects under the supervision of practicing lawyers and law school faculty. Law school clinical programs might include work in legal aid clinics, for example, or on the staff of legislative committees. Part-time or summer clerkships in law firms, government agencies, and corporate legal departments also provide experience that can be extremely valuable later. Such training can provide job references or lead directly to a job after graduation, and it can help students decide what kind of practice best suits them. Clerkships also may be an important source of financial aid.

Graduates receive the degree of juris doctor (J.D.) or bachelor of law (LL.B.) as the first professional degree. Advanced law degrees may be desirable for those planning to specialize, do research, or teach. Some law students pursue joint degree programs, which generally require an additional year of study. Joint degree programs are offered in a number of areas, including law and business administration and law and public administration.

After graduation, lawyers must keep informed about legal and nonlegal developments that affect their practice. Thirty-seven states and jurisdictions mandate Continuing Legal Education (CLE). Furthermore, many law schools and state and local bar associations provide continuing education courses that help lawyers stay abreast of recent developments.

The practice of law involves a great deal of responsibility. Persons planning careers in law should like to work with people and be able to win the respect and confidence of their clients, associates, and the public. Integrity and honesty are vital personal qualities. Perseverance and reasoning ability are essential for analyzing complex cases and reaching sound conclusions. Lawyers also need creativity when handling new and unique legal problems.

Most beginning lawyers start in salaried positions. Newly hired salaried attorneys usually act as research assistants to experienced lawyers or judges. After several years of salaried employment involving progressively more responsiblity, some lawyers are admitted to partnership in their firms or go into practice for themselves. Some lawyers, after years of practice, become full-time law school faculty members or administrators; a growing number have advanced degrees in other fields as well.

Some persons use their legal training in administrative or managerial positions in various departments of large corporations. Transferring from a corporation's legal department to another department often is viewed as a way to gain administrative experience and rise in the ranks of management.

TRAINING FOR JUDGES

Most judges have worked as lawyers. All federal judges and state trial and appellate court judges are required to be lawyers or learned in law. About forty states presently allow non-lawyers to hold limited jurisdiction judgeships, but opportunities are better with law experience.

Federal administrative law judges must be lawyers and pass a competitive examination administered by the U.S. Office of Personnel Management. Many state administrative law judges and other hearing officials are not required to be lawyers, but law degrees are preferred for most positions.

Federal judges are appointed for life by the president, with the consent of the Senate. Federal administrative law judges are appointed by the various federal agencies and are given lifetime tenure. About half of all state judges are appointed, while the remainder are elected in partisan or nonpartisan state elections.

Most state and local judges serve fixed terms, which range from four or six years for most limited jurisdiction judgeships to as long as fourteen years for some appellate court judges. Judicial nominating commissions, composed of members of the bar and the public, are used to screen candidates for judgeships in many states as well as for federal judgeships.

All states have some type of orientation for newly elected or appointed judges. Thirteen states also require judges to take continuing education courses while serving on the bench.

JOB OUTLOOK

Lawyers and judges held about 735,000 jobs in 1994. About three-fourths of the 656,000 lawyers practiced privately, either in law firms or in individual practice. Most of the remaining lawyers held positions in government, the greatest number at the local level.

In the federal government, lawyers are concentrated in the departments of Justice, Treasury, and Defense, but they work for other federal agencies as well. Other lawyers are employed as house counsel by public utilities, banks, insurance companies, real estate agencies, manufacturing firms, welfare and religious organizations, and other business firms and nonprofit organizations.

Some salaried lawyers also have part-time independent practices; others work as lawyers part time while working full time in other occupations.

Persons seeking positions as lawyers or judges should encounter keen competition through the year 2005. Law schools still attract large numbers of applicants, and they are not expected to decrease their enrollments, so the supply of persons trained as lawyers should continue to exceed job openings.

Employment of lawyers has grown very rapidly since the early 1970s and is expected to continue to grow faster than the average for all occupations through the year 2005. New jobs created by this growth should exceed the job openings that arise from the need to replace lawyers who stop working or leave the profession. The strong growth in demand for lawyers will result from growth in the population and the general level of business activities. Demand also will be spurred by growth of legal action in such areas as employee benefits, consumer protection, criminal prosecution, the environment, and finance and by an anticipated increase in the use of legal services by middle-income groups through legal clinics and prepaid legal service programs.

Even though jobs for lawyers are expected to increase rapidly, competition for job openings should continue to be keen because of the large numbers graduating from law school each year.

During the 1970s, the annual number of law school graduates more than doubled, outpacing the rapid growth of jobs. Growth in the yearly number of law school graduates tapered off during the 1980s but again increased in the early 1990s. The high number of graduates will strain the economy's capacity to absorb them. Although graduates with superior academic records from well-regarded law schools will continue to enjoy good opportunities, most graduates will encounter competition for jobs. As in the past, some graduates may have to accept positions in areas outside their fields of interest or for which they feel they are overqualified. They may have to enter jobs for which legal training is an asset but not normally a requirement. For example, banks, insurance firms, real estate companies, government agencies, and other organizations seek law graduates to fill many administrative, managerial, and business positions.

Due to the competition for jobs, a law school graduate's geographic mobility and work experience assume greater importance. The willingness to relocate may be an advantage in getting a job, but to be licensed in a new state, a lawyer may have to take an additional state bar examination. In addition, employers increasingly seek graduates who have advanced law degrees and experience in a particular field such as tax, patent, or admiralty law.

Employment growth of lawyers will continue to be concentrated in salaried jobs, as businesses and all levels of government employ a growing number of staff attorneys and as employment in the legal services industry is increasingly concentrated in larger law firms.

The number of self-employed lawyers is expected to increase only slowly, reflecting the difficulty of establishing a profitable new practice in the face of competition from larger, established law firms. Also, the growing complexity of law, which encourages specialization, and the cost of maintaining up-to-date legal research materials both favor larger firms.

For lawyers who nevertheless wish to work independently, establishing a new practice probably will continue to be easiest in small towns and expanding suburban areas, as long as an active market for legal services already exists. In such communities, competition from larger established law firms is likely to be less than in big cities, and new lawyers may find it easier to become known to potential clients; also, rent and other business costs are somewhat lower. Nevertheless, starting a new practice will remain an expensive and risky undertaking that should be weighed carefully.

Most salaried positions will remain in urban areas where government agencies, law firms, and big corporations are concentrated.

Some lawyers are adversely affected by cyclical swings in the economy. During recessions, the demand for some discretionary legal services, such as planning estates, drafting wills, and handling real estate transactions, declines. Also, corporations are less likely to litigate cases when declining sales and profits result in budgetary restrictions. Although few lawyers actually lose their jobs during these times, earnings may decline for many. Some corporations and law firms will not hire new attorneys until business improves. Several factors, however, mitigate the overall impact of recessions on lawyers. During recessions, individuals and corporations face other legal problems, such as bankruptcies, foreclosures, and divorces, that require legal action. Furthermore, new laws and legal interpretations create new opportunities for lawyers.

The prestige associated with serving on the bench should ensure continued intense competition for openings. Employment of judges is expected to grow more slowly than the average for all occupations. Contradictory social forces affect the demand for judges. Pushing up demand are public concerns about crime, safety, and efficient administration of justice; on the other hand, tight public funding should slow job growth.

Competition for judgeships should remain keen. Most job openings will arise as judges retire. Traditionally, many judges have held their positions until late in life. Now, early retirement is becoming more common, creating more job openings; however, becoming a judge will still be difficult. Besides competing with other qualified people, judicial candidates must gain political support in order to be elected or appointed.

SALARIES FOR ATTORNEYS

Annual salaries of beginning lawyers in private industry averaged about $37,000 in 1993, but some top graduates from the nation's best law schools started at over $80,000 a year.

In the federal government, annual starting salaries for attorneys in 1994 were about $29,200 or $36,400, depending upon academic and personal qualifications.

Factors affecting the salaries offered to new graduates include academic record; type, size, and location of employer; and specialized educational background. The field of law makes a difference, too. Patent lawyers, for example, generally are among the highest-paid attorneys.

Salaries of experienced attorneys also vary widely according to the types, sizes, and locations of their employers. The average salary of the most experienced lawyers in private industry in 1993 was nearly $115,000, but some senior lawyers who were partners in the nation's top law firms earned over $1 million.

General attorneys in the federal government averaged around $67,900 a year in 1995; the relatively few patent attorneys in the federal government averaged around $76,300.

Lawyers on salary receive increases as they assume greater responsibility. Lawyers starting their own practice may need to work part time in other occupations during the first years to supplement their incomes. Their incomes usually grow as their practices develop. Lawyers who are partners in law firms generally earn more than those who practice alone.

Most salaried lawyers and judges are provided health and life insurance, and contributions are made on their behalf to retirement plans. Lawyers who practice independently are only covered if they arrange and pay for such benefits themselves.

SALARIES FOR JUDGES

Federal district court judges had salaries of $133,600 in 1995, as did judges in the Court of Federal Claims. Circuit court judges earned $141,700 a year. Federal judges with limited jurisdiction, such as magistrates and bankruptcy court judges, had salaries of $122,900 in 1995. Full-time federal administrative law judges received average salaries of $94,800 in 1995. The Chief Justice of the U.S. Supreme Court earned $171,500 in 1995, and the Associate Justices earned $164,100.

Annual salaries of associate justices of the states' highest courts in 1995 averaged $91,093 and ranged from about $64,452 to $131,085, according to a survey by the National Center for State Courts.

Salaries of state intermediate appellate court judges in 1995 averaged $91,093 but ranged from $64,452 to $131,085. Salaries of state judges with limited jurisdiction varied widely; many such salaries are set locally.

RELATED FIELDS
Attorneys

Legal training is useful in many occupations besides law occupations. Paralegals, arbitrators, journalists, patent agents, title examiners, legislative assistants, lobbyists, FBI special agents, political office holders, and corporate executives are among the people who find legal training helpful as they carry out their duties.

Judges

The skills a judge must possess are useful to people in many other occupations, such as arbitrators, legislators, lobbyists, political office holders, and corporate executives.

INTERVIEW
Diane B. Camerlo
In-House Counsel

Diane B. Camerlo works with four other lawyers in the legal department of the Federal Reserve Bank of St. Louis. She received her B.A. from Denison University, in Granville, Ohio, with a double major in sociology and English. In 1976, she earned her J.D. from Franklin Pierce Law Center in Concord, New Hampshire. She has been practicing for more than twenty years.

What the Job Is Really Like

"The Federal Reserve Bank of St. Louis is one of the twelve operating arms of the Federal Reserve System located throughout the nation that, together with their twenty-five branches, carry out various system functions, including operating a nationwide payments system, distributing the nation's currency and coin, supervising and regulating member banks and bank holding companies, and serving as banker for the U.S. Treasury.

"My day is usually made up of some combination of meetings, client counseling, research, writing, planning, public speaking, telephone calls, traveling, and administrative duties. I could spend an entire day doing any one of those things, or I could do all of those things during the course of the day. I also attend Continuing Legal Education seminars from time to time and serve on business-related committees and task forces.

"In my law department the lawyers don't have rigidly defined areas of specialization, so each of us works on a wide variety of projects. The areas of law that might be involved include employment, employee benefits, contract, commercial, intellectual property, banking, general corporate, antitrust, environmental, safety, technology, tax, litigation, or just about anything else. Most of my work involves contracts, employment, banking, or technology law. I also review bank holding-company applications required to be filed with the Federal Reserve. And we also monitor pending federal and state legislation that affects our industry.

"I am usually very busy with twenty or more active projects going on at one time. During the week I work nine to ten hours on a typical day, though I sometimes work a much longer (or occasionally shorter) day.

"The atmosphere in my law department is businesslike and friendly. The lawyers usually work on individual projects, but we frequently confer with each other. This give and take between attorneys enables us to provide better legal advice to our clients and also makes the job more rewarding.

"I like the intellectual challenge and stimulation of practicing law. I like working in a corporation where I can understand the business in depth and work with the businesspeople to achieve the corporation's goals. I also enjoy the supportive atmosphere in our legal department.

"The primary downside to practicing law is the high level of pressure. Lawyers must give accurate legal advice, often with very short time limits. Another downside is the confrontational nature of the legal practice. Fortunately, this is much less a factor in an in-house corporate practice than in a law firm practice. Finally, the low opinion of lawyers by the general public is sometimes hard to take. While there are some bad apples in the legal profession, as in all professions, in my law department we place a high value on ethical behavior and client service."

How Diane Camerlo Got Started

"When I graduated from college with a B.A. in sociology and English, I realized my career choices were limited to low-level jobs that would only lead to careers that didn't interest me. I considered various graduate school options and chose law because I believed lawyers did interesting, challenging work and were well paid and highly respected. My father had practiced law before taking a business position, so the field was familiar to me.

"In 1976 I began working as an associate in a law firm in Toledo, Ohio, and then later became a partner. The firm had about thirty-five to forty-five lawyers. I practiced mostly antitrust law, including complex litigation, but when Reagan dried up antitrust I did workers' comp. That was the pits after antitrust, so later I quit and moved to Rochester, New York, and sold computers until my daughter was born. I then took a law/business/computer job with a former legal client (a bank), and then I took a job in the Monsanto corporate legal department doing antitrust and general corporate work. I was only a contractor in that job (i.e., I had no benefits) so when the Fed job opened up, I took it. Thus, I've had experience in just about every way a lawyer can have experience except as a prosecutor, public defender, or judge."

Expert Advice

"For anyone considering a career in law I would recommend going to the best law school possible and getting the highest grades possible. Grades are especially important. The market for new lawyers is tight and those with low grades will have more trouble getting a job than those with high grades."

● ● ●

INTERVIEW
Joseph Tringali
Assistant State Attorney General

Joseph Tringali has been an attorney since 1970. He earned both his B.A. in history and his J.D. at the State University of New York, Buffalo. He joined the staff of the attorney general's office in Palm Beach County, Florida, in 1990.

What the Job Is Really Like

"The attorney general of any state is the chief law officer of the state. In Florida in the attorney general's office there are probably 200 assistant attorneys general in offices in various cities statewide. We represent the state in civil actions—for example, in the big tobacco lawsuit that's going on now.

"I'm not involved in that, though. I handle criminal appeals on behalf of the state. When these criminals, who are convicted beyond a reasonable doubt and are sent off to prison, where they richly deserve to be, appeal and attempt to get out, it's my job to keep them in.

"In some states the local prosecutors have an appellate division in each office. Our state has elected the system of having all appellate cases handled by the attorney general.

"Although my job title is different, I function similarly to prosecuting attorneys. In New York State, for example, I was an assistant district attorney and our office handled both prosecuting cases and the appeals.

"Appellate law is a much more esoteric practice and much less stressful than trial law. In a trial situation you are the key player especially if you are the prosecutor. It's up to you to have the witnesses there on time, it's up to you to call them in the order you need them. You're the maestro—you're conducting the orchestra.

"In my job I'm in court very rarely. Generally speaking I handle a lot of drug cases, a lot of homicide cases. The appellant is bringing the action so the first thing that happens is that I get a brief from the defendant's attorney. He says there were all these legal errors at the trial. I read the brief, then I might spend one to three days reading the transcript of the trial, looking to see if things happened the way he said they did. Sometimes things can be interpreted differently. Then I'll research the case law, other appellate cases on those legal issues. Then I write a brief in opposition, called an *answer brief*, on behalf of the state. The appellant gets to write what is called a *reply brief*. Then all the briefs get filed in the appellate court.

The appellate judge and his or her law clerks then study that. Although my position is similar to that of a law clerk working with an appellate judge, he or she is supposed to be impartial. I'm an advocate for the state. The law clerk is neutral; I'm trying to find ways to uphold the conviction.

"After the judge goes over the briefs, 90 percent of the time nothing else happens. The appellate court will either affirm the conviction without comment or they will write an opinion either affirming or reversing. If it gets reversed, usually it means that the state has to retry the case.

"Every once in a while, one side or the other will request an oral argument. That's when we get to go to court and give an oral presentation. There's a great difference of opinion on whether oral arguments actually do the appellant any good. During my first oral argument I was in there heating up the courtroom, with the old trial lawyer instincts coming out, and one of the judges said to me, 'Counselor, you can relax. There's no jury here.' In other words, there's nobody to impress here with theatrics. The judges know the law and all you need to do is make your point intellectually and then sit down.

"I get to make an oral argument maybe once a month or once every six weeks. It's the part of my work I enjoy the most.

"I honestly prefer the work I'm doing now to trial lawyering. This is the pure practice of law without the personalities or the peculiarities of any particular trial judges. You don't have to worry about whether witnesses will show up or whether they'll be good or bad witnesses. When you're a prosecuting attorney it feels more like playing *Let's Make a Deal*. It's easy to get burned out.

"My job is law as an intellectual exercise."

How Joseph Tringali Got Started

"I was always interested in the idea of government and I was attracted by trial law in particular, the drama of the courtroom. Maybe I should have been an actor. This was the era of *Perry Mason*, and everyone saw that on television. But I also spent quite a bit of time in downtown Buffalo when I was in high school and even later when I was in college. I would go into the courthouse and actually watch the trials as they were going on. And of course the reality is a lot different from *Perry Mason*. I would hang around and see the lawyers rushing to and fro in the hallways. Probably the most dramatic scenes take place there rather than in the courtrooms. That's where the lawyers are huddling with their clients and explaining the facts of legal life.

"After I graduated law school, I worked in Buffalo as an assistant district attorney for two years; then I came down to Palm Beach County in Florida as an assistant state attorney. It was the same job as in New York but with a different title. I stayed for three years and then went back to Buffalo and worked as assistant corporation counsel for two years, representing the city of Buffalo, and did labor law cases. Then I went into private practice for fourteen years, handling all sorts of cases—criminal, family, anything that came through the door.

"In 1990 I came back to Florida and took my present job working for the attorney general."

Expert Advice

"Law is a much more demanding profession than most people realize. I think that anyone who enters it should be aware that it is not the *Perry Mason*, television/movie kind of thing. Nor is it the high income profession everyone thinks it is across the board. Yes, there are a lot of attorneys out there earning a lot of money. But there are also attorneys running themselves ragged from courtroom to courtroom, earning less than I do—and I earn only $45,500 a year.

"Don't go out and buy the Mercedes just yet."

●   ●   ●

INTERVIEW
Barbara F. Arrants
Public Defender

Barbara Arrants earned her B.S. in psychology in 1985 from the University of the South, Sewanee, Tennessee, and her J.D. from the University of Tennessee, Knoxville, in 1991.

What the Job Is Really Like

"I worked for four years for the Davidson County Metropolitan Public Defender's Office in Nashville, Tennessee. I started as a general sessions attorney, handling misdemeanor trials and bind-over hearings, then worked as a criminal court attorney (on felony trials), and then I was named lead trial attorney for DUI court, which covered DUI, vehicular homicide, and aggravated assault trials and hearings.

"One of the first things I ever did at the PD's office was investigate a triple homicide. I had to review the crime scene photos and autopsies and then do extensive interviews with the defendant and his family. I could've written a book on how to create a killer!

"A public defender's life is thrilling, exciting, stressful, thankless, impossible, and wonderful—all rolled into one. I worked forty-five to fifty-five hours a week. As a general sessions attorney I would walk into court every morning, court docket in hand, with some fifteen to twenty-five names highlighted. These were my clients for the day, many of whom I would meet for the first time. Needless to say, you have to be able to think on your feet. I would meet and talk with each of my clients for a few minutes and then go into the courtroom for the call of the docket. After docket call, I met with the district attorneys. As a result of this meeting I marked some cases for trial, some for a bond reduction hearing, some for plea bargain offers, and some for bind-over hearings. I stayed in court all day until all of the cases were disposed of. I handled all of the hearings, trials, and pleas that day. This goes on every day, five days a week. All of the trials are bench trials (judge only) unless the client requests otherwise. If a client requests a jury trial, the case is bound over to the grand jury.

"Criminal court is not quite so hectic, but the cases are more serious and the trials are almost always in front of a jury. I was actually in court about three days a week: two days for trials, sometimes longer, and one day for motions and hearings. I handled every aspect of a client's felony case: arraignment, research, investigation, pretrial motions, bond issues, and trial.

"DUI court was the same. I handled DUIs set for jury trial (i.e., they were not settled/tried in general sessions court), vehicular homicide, and aggravated assault (with a vehicle). As DUI attorney, I was in charge of approximately 200 active cases, including probation violations. I was in court two to three days a week for trials, hearings, and motions. I averaged a jury trial per week.

"The work atmosphere is high-pressure, confrontational, and intense but very exciting. What I liked most was the enormous amount of courtroom work. If you like litigation, it's the place to be.

"What I disliked was fighting the stereotype that a PD is a lousy lawyer simply because he or she works for indigent clients. In fact, in most cases, the opposite is true. Most of the PDs I know are exceptional attorneys. Like me, they graduated in the top part of their class and do this type of work because they enjoy it, not because they couldn't get any other job.

"The only difference between a PD and a hired attorney is the amount of money available for expert witnesses, tests, exhibits, and the like. The other difference is the huge workload a public defender handles. A private attorney will have one client for the day; I may have twenty! The quality of the attorney is essentially the same, however.

"Now, I am no longer working as a public defender. I am in private practice, but truthfully I am home with young children. I will return to criminal practice full-time in a few years. I found it very difficult to keep up the relentless pace of PD work and be a mother. Sometimes I would have to go across town in the middle of the night for an interview or downtown to the Criminal Justice Center for a lineup or interrogation. I decided that while my children were young, I needed to stay home for a few years. I really miss the work, but it was difficult on my family."

How Barbara Arrants Got Started

"I went to law school because—let's face it—a liberal arts degree means I have a good education but no qualifications for anything!

"While applying for law school and taking the LSATs, I worked as a runner for a large firm here in Nashville. I became acquainted with all the different types of law there are, what one actually *did* as a lawyer, and so forth. I came away with the feeling that I did not want to be an associate in a firm. All associates do is the partners' paperwork. That did not appeal to me at all. I wanted to be in the thick of things!

"During my first year at law school I attended the mock trial competition (held every year in every law school nationwide). That's all it took. I took a trial advocacy course my second year and blew my professor away—got the highest grade in the class. He told me that litigation was where I needed to be.

"Criminal law appeals to me because of my psych background—what makes people do the things they do? Why does someone become a criminal?

"I could have been a prosecutor or a defense attorney—I fell into the defense side simply because someone told me the PDs were always looking for interns. I interned with them and they offered me a job before I had finished my second year. Never one to look a gift horse in the mouth, I jumped on it."

Expert Advice

"If you are interested in litigation, a job as a public defender or district attorney gets you more experience at a faster pace than any other career choice. If you start your career with a firm, you can expect to wait as long as five years before you see the inside of a courtroom. I handled my first bench trial the first week I was working! It is incredibly demanding but very rewarding as well."

●   ●   ●

INTERVIEW
John Wiorek
Law Clerk

John Wiorek graduated law school summa cum laude and was editor of the Law Review. *He works for an appellate judge in the Third District Illinois Appellate Court.*

What the Job Is Really Like

"*Law clerk* isn't a title I'm particularly fond of. It makes people think you work in a grocery store or something. If I could change the job title, I'd call it something along the lines of *research attorney.* Sometimes we're called *elbow clerks* because we work at the elbow of the judge.

"Duties will vary depending on the judge you work with. In my case, writing and research are my primary duties. Every month we have court call. We handle both civil and criminal appeals. People have been to trial and, for one reason or another, they don't like the results so they file an appeal. They submit written arguments—called *briefs*—and we get copies of those arguments. In the month that a person's case is scheduled to go before the court, we're sent the briefs. We're also sent the record—that is, the transcripts and common law record of all the proceedings.

"In Illinois each appellate judge gets two law clerks. So usually the other clerk and I will split up the work.

"We know what cases are set for the particular month and we have all these stacks of briefs to read. The three of us— myself, the other law clerk, and the judge—make notes on the briefs and arguments. This could take three or four days.

"Then we have a conference and go through each case and discuss it. We give the judge our ideas on how the case should turn out.

"At the same time, we begin to research the law regarding those cases. We might work up a rough draft of decisions and do bench memos for other cases—giving a brief synopsis of the arguments and the law and what our feelings are about what the decision should or shouldn't be.

"The judge will listen to the oral arguments and come back and tell us what was decided, whether it was affirmed or reversed, and he or she will explain the reasons for how the decision was reached. We will then write a draft of the order.

"Any stress on the job would be mostly self-imposed. There are no hard and fast deadlines, although you do have to produce a certain amount of work in a certain amount of time. No judge likes to get behind in his or her case load.

"Sometimes the work can get a bit repetitious—the issues can recur and they can be boring. Sometimes you read a 2,000-page transcript and you're sitting there for three days reading some psychiatrist's opinion about someone's sanity and going through the results of his or her MMPI and different psychological tests. It can get tedious.

"I like most the low level of stress and that it is nine to five—which gives me the opportunity to do other things. I teach a night course in criminal law at Western Illinois and I can handle things on the side for clients if I want to.

"Plus, there is a certain satisfaction when you're done with a case, especially if they decide to make it an opinion rather than an order—which means it will be published. You can see in the books that you made a small contribution to developing the law.

"I wouldn't mind staying in this work, but I'm also considering full-time teaching as well. I get quite a kick out of it.

"Right now I earn around $44,000. The position at the college would start at $36,000 and it would be a bit of a step down, at least initially. Private practice would pay more, but money isn't the biggest thing. The most important thing is to have control of your lifestyle."

How John Wiorek Got Started

"My decision to go into law came primarily from finding out after graduating with a bachelor's in psychology that the options were fairly limited with that kind of degree. So I spent some time kicking around a little bit, trying to decide the best route to go—a Ph.D. in psychology or law school. Although I had no great burning desire to go into law, law school seemed like the best option, something I'd be good at—based on my LSAT results—and something I thought had a fairly good potential for a job.

"I got my B.S. from Western Illinois University in Macomb in 1978. I attended law school at Southern Illinois University in Carbondale and finished in 1988 with a J.D.

"When I first got out of law school I worked as a staff attorney on the Fifth District Appellate Court in Mount Vernon, Illinois. Then, after six months, I started clerking for Judge Chapman, and I worked for him for around two years. I started in my current position with Judge Kent Slater in December of 1990.

"Most of the time law clerk positions are temporary; one or two years is the norm. It is more seen as a stepping stone to something else rather than a career in itself. In fact the reason I no longer work for the first judge is that he basically said to me, okay, your two years are up and it's time for you to move on to something else. He thought I should be doing something 'better' for my career. I chose to continue as a law clerk with another judge because I found that I liked this kind of work, that I was good at it and I was comfortable with it. I didn't want to work with a firm. There are so many horror stories. The eighty-hour weeks. The grind. It didn't appeal to me at all.

"My job is nine to five. You get a steady paycheck, you know how much it's going to be, you don't work weekends or nights, and the stress level is really low."

Expert Advice

"There are certain qualifications you have to have. If you want to be a law clerk, you're going to have to finish in at least the top quarter or probably the top 10 percent of your class. They're going to want you to have those good grades or be on *Law Review*.

"Also, you have to be able to write and like to write. If it's a real chore for you, it won't be the right job for you. Your analytical skills have to be fairly high, too.

"I would advise anyone to be a law clerk for at least one to two years. If you're thinking about making it a career, there are a couple of things to keep in mind. You'll make less money than in a firm. Plus, the job security isn't there. You serve at the whim of the judge you work for. He or she could retire or quit or not get reelected and then you're out of a job.

"Another point is to make sure you take a job with a judge you like and get along with. You spend a lot of time working closely together, so that's important. I'm lucky. I have a good judge to work for."

● ● ●

INTERVIEW
James Lanuti
Circuit Judge

James Lanuti earned his J.D. at IIT, the Illinois Institute of Technology, at Chicago Kent College of Law in 1977. He is now a judge in the circuit court of LaSalle County in Illinois.

What the Job Is Really Like

"I hear civil cases. I have divorce cases on my docket, I have paternity cases, I have lawsuits, personal injury cases, contract disputes. The lawsuits range in size from $2,500 all the way up to million-dollar suits. And I also handle some probate matters, estates, will contests, that sort of thing.

"I've handled just about everything. When I first went on the bench I did a lot of divorce cases. Then I spent four years doing traffic court, where I heard the traffic cases as well as all the drunk driving cases, the serious traffic cases as well as reckless homicide cases, where people have been killed in drunk driving accidents, and some felonies—people charged with more serious crimes.

"At the same time I also heard the cases that are the most distressing—juvenile cases. I was the presiding judge of the juvenile court, where I heard all the juvenile delinquency cases as well as cases involving abused and neglected children. I did that about four years. Than I came back and did another stretch of civil cases. I was also in charge of the probate court for a while.

"In 1992 I was assigned to go to criminal court, and I spent about three and half years there. I just came to civil court about a month ago—at my request. I was ready for a little change. I heard only murder cases, armed robbery, and so forth. It would be ideal to get a variety of criminal and civil cases, but in my county we separate the two.

"My caseload varies from day to day. If everything was litigated you couldn't hear more than one case in a day. In an average day you might have thirty cases on your docket, but they all go away because they get settled. On another day you might only have half a dozen on the docket, but that might be a day you're in court all day because the cases are contested.

"We have juries come in on Mondays and we schedule all our jury trials on that day. If we need more time, we can do it on Tuesday and Wednesday. It doesn't usually take longer than a day to pick a jury, unless it's a big murder case. Then it can take more and we have to make special arrangements for that.

"A lot of times the only incentive to settle is that the case is going to be called. It's almost brinkmanship in negotiating some of these cases. The jury has to be there and ready to go before the parties will settle.

"The rest of the week we get more involved cases and we're very busy.

"I'm in here by 8:00 or 8:30 to get ready for the day. My first court call is at 9:00. If the cases resolve themselves I can sometimes finish in court at 3:00, but if not I'll be here until 5:00.

"When I finish court early, I can use the time in chambers to familiarize myself with the next day's call. When I was a lawyer, I always appreciated a judge who took the time to read the papers that the lawyers had filed and be prepared. That isn't always the case, but that's one thing as a judge I've always shot for, and to do it requires a certain amount of homework. You have to read the files, read the motions and the answers, and do some research.

"We don't have interns or law clerks, but we do have a circuit clerk who is basically the recordkeeper and does the scheduling, like a clerk of the court. We do our own research.

"Obviously, the work is very interesting. It's not boring at all and you see a lot of situations where you think you can make a difference. You can't always make everyone happy, though. Your first and foremost job is to follow the law. Sometimes that's not popular, but as long as you can do it consistently it will give you a sense of satisfaction. You're doing your part to administer justice.

"It can be frustrating sometimes if you end up having to hear cases that really should have been resolved before they came to court. You see a lot of people who are almost self-destructive. I see that a lot in divorce cases, like the movie *The War of the Roses*. That's not totally untrue. And the saddest thing about it is the effect it has on children. That's one of the things we've tried to focus on in recent years in the court system on a national level. What can the courts do to make sure the children don't get lost in the shuffle? You have to realize, though, that the litigants have ultimate control over their own lives. You can't solve all of society's social problems. Even though you'd like to be able to get people to listen, sometimes they won't take your advice.

"It's also frustrating to see a juvenile come in, charged with a crime. You try to work with him—you talk to him, maybe give him probation and all sorts of other services. It's sad to see him come back a couple of years later charged with a felony as an adult and he's going to go to prison.

"Once in a while you might worry about a decision on a tough case, but not often. I've felt comfortable with most of the decisions I've made. You have to have the ability to put the case behind you or else you won't be effective."

How James Lanuti Got Started

"I got my B.S. in math at the University of Illinois in 1969 and then worked as a computer program systems analyst for seven years. In fact, I worked while I went to law school at night. My goal at the time was to be able to work for myself and be independent, and I saw the law as a way to do that. I never intended at the time I started law school to become a judge. That was never a goal.

"I worked for a firm in Chicago for a couple of years and then I came to Ottawa because I had relatives in this area. My uncle is a lawyer here, and in 1979 I went to work with him.

"I also started working for the state's attorney office as a part-time assistant state attorney. I handled civil matters and represented the county government in county cases at the same time I was practicing law privately.

"The way the system works in the state of Illinois is that we have two levels of trial judges: associate judges and circuit judges. The associate judges are appointed by the circuit judges, for four-year terms. The circuit judges are elected for six-year terms. The circuit judges have to run for retention on a yes/no ballot every six years.

"In 1986, there was a judicial vacancy for an associate judge, and I talked about it with my family, and I thought, why not give it a try? If I don't get it, I won't look back and worry about it. But I got appointed.

"Whenever there's a vacancy for an associate judge, a notice is posted at the courthouse and any lawyer can apply. Then all the circuit judges meet and vote via secret ballot.

"I knew the circuit judges at that point. That's one of the strong points of the system. The same lawyers that apply appear in the courtroom in front of the same judges who vote, so the judges already have a pretty good idea of the capabilities of the lawyer."

Expert Advice

"I don't think you start off considering a career as a judge. First, you have to decide if you want to get into the law and if you want to be a lawyer; that's a career you choose. Once you're practicing law, you know more about it and know if that's what you want to do.

"Some people are designed to be advocates—they can advocate a position strongly even though the position might not be a good one. They don't judge their own clients. The client comes in and says, 'This is the position I want to take in this case,' and the lawyer says, 'It's not unreasonable; let's go ahead with it.' Other lawyers, though, might be more judgmental. They might say, 'Come on, Mr. Client, we'll never sell this to the jury. Let's compromise.' You see the practical route and the outcome and you're not wearing blinders just to advocate your client's position. If that's the way you operate, it might be an indication that you're better off being a judge.

"Being a judge has its advantages and disadvantages over being a lawyer. The advantage is that it is a somewhat prestigious position and you have respect in the community. Lawyers are often the victims of jokes, but judges are highly respected. It's amazing to me how a lawyer becomes extremely wise once he or she becomes a judge.

"It's a steady position, you'll make a good living and you have a certain amount of freedom in the job: you're in charge of your docket and you're the one making the decisions, you can have some control with what's going on in front of you with the lawyers, and you get the holidays and the weekends off.

"But the idea of being your own boss is something you have to give up when you're a judge because now you're a public servant. You're no longer working for yourself; you're working for the public, and you have an obligation to be at work and be on the job.

"And though you do make a good living, you are giving up the opportunity to make substantially more as a lawyer. There are lawyers, obviously, who don't make as much money as judges, but there are a lot of lawyers who make a lot more."

●   ●   ●

FOR MORE INFORMATION

The American Bar Association annually publishes the *Review of Legal Education in the United States*, which provides detailed information on each of the 177 law schools approved by the ABA, state requirements for admission to legal practice, a directory of state bar examination administrators, and other information on legal education. Single copies are free from the ABA, but there is a fee for multiple copies. Free information on the bar examination, financial aid for law students, and law as a career may also be obtained from

> Member Services
> American Bar Association
> 541 North Fairbanks Court
> Chicago, IL 60611-3314

Information on the LSAT, the Law School Data Assembly Service, applying to law school, and financial aid for law students may be obtained from

> Law School Admission Services
> P.O. Box 40
> Newtown, PA 18940

The specific requirements for admission to the bar in a particular state or other jurisdiction may also be obtained at the state capital, from the clerk of the Supreme Court, or from the administrator of the State Board of Bar Examiners.

3 # Police Work

EDUCATION
H.S. degree required;
   B.A./B.S. preferred

$$$ SALARY
$18,000–$59,000

OVERVIEW

The safety of our nation's cities, towns, and highways greatly depends on the work of police officers, deputy sheriffs, detectives, and special agents, whose responsibilities range from controlling traffic to preventing and investigating crimes. In most jurisdictions, these officers, whether on or off duty, are expected to exercise their authority whenever necessary.

As civilian police department employees and private security personnel increasingly assume routine police duties, police and detectives are able to spend more time fighting serious crime. Police and detectives are also becoming more involved in community relations, increasing public confidence in the police and mobilizing the public to help the police fight crime.

Police officers and detectives who work in small communities and rural areas have many duties. In the course of a day's work, they may direct traffic at the scene of a fire, investigate a burglary, or give first aid to an accident victim. In a large police department, by contrast, officers usually are assigned to a specific type of duty. Most officers are detailed either to patrol or to traffic duty; some are assigned to special work such as accident prevention. Others are experts in chemical and microscopic analysis, firearms identification, and handwriting and fingerprint identification. In very large cities, a few officers may work with special units such as mounted and motorcycle police, harbor patrols, helicopter patrols, canine corps, mobile rescue teams, and youth aid services.

Sheriffs and deputy sheriffs generally enforce the law in rural areas or those places where there is no local police department. Bailiffs are responsible for keeping order in the courtroom. U.S. marshals serve civil writs and criminal warrants issued by federal judges and are responsible for the safety and transportation of jurors and prisoners.

Detectives and special agents are plainclothes investigators who gather facts and collect evidence for criminal cases. They conduct interviews, examine records, observe the activities of suspects, and participate in raids and arrests.

Federal Bureau of Investigation (FBI) special agents investigate violations of federal laws in connection with bank robberies, theft of government property, organized crime, espionage, sabotage, kidnapping, and terrorism. Agents with specialized training usually work on cases related to their backgrounds. For example, an agent with an accounting background may investigate white-collar crimes such as bank embezzlements or fraudulent bankruptcies and land deals. Frequently, agents must testify in court about cases that they investigate.

Special agents employed by the U.S. Department of Treasury work for the U.S. Customs Service; the Bureau of Alcohol, Tobacco, and Firearms; the U.S. Secret Service; and the Internal Revenue Service. Customs agents enforce laws to prevent smuggling of goods across U.S. borders. Alcohol, Tobacco, and Firearms agents might investigate suspected illegal sales of guns or the underpayment of taxes by a liquor or cigarette manufacturer. U.S. Secret Service agents protect the president, vice president, and their immediate families; presidential candidates; ex-presidents; and foreign dignitaries visiting the United States. Secret Service agents also investigate counterfeiting, the forgery of government checks or bonds, and the fraudulent use of credit cards. Internal Revenue Service special agents collect evidence against individuals and companies that are neglecting to pay federal taxes.

Federal drug enforcement agents conduct criminal investigations of illicit drug activity. They compile evidence and arrest individuals who violate federal drug laws. They may prepare reports that are used in criminal proceedings, give testimony in court, and develop evidence that justifies the seizure of financial assets gained from illegal activity.

State police officers (sometimes called state troopers or highway patrol officers) patrol highways and enforce laws and regulations that govern their use. They issue traffic citations to motorists who violate the law. At the scene of an accident, they direct traffic, give first aid, and call for emergency equipment, including ambulances. They also write reports that may be used to determine the causes of accidents. In addition, state police officers provide services to motorists on the highways. For example, they may radio for road service for drivers with mechanical trouble, direct tourists to their destinations, or give information about lodging, restaurants, and tourist attractions.

State police officers also provide traffic assistance and control during road repairs, fires, and other emergencies as well as during special occurrences such as parades and sports events. They sometimes check the weight of commercial vehicles, conduct driver examinations, and give information on highway safety to the public.

In addition to having highway responsibilities, state police in the majority of states also enforce criminal laws. In communities and counties that do not have local police forces or large sheriffs' departments, the state police are the primary law enforcement agency, investigating crimes such as burglary or assault. They also may help city or county police catch law-breakers and control civil disturbances.

Most new police recruits begin on patrol duty, riding in a police vehicle or walking on foot patrol. They work alone or with experienced officers in such varied areas as congested business districts or outlying residential neighborhoods. Officers attempt to become thoroughly familiar with conditions throughout their areas and, while on patrol, remain alert for anything unusual. They note suspicious circumstances, such as open windows or lights in vacant buildings, as well as hazards to public safety such as burned-out street lights or fallen trees. Officers enforce traffic regulations and also watch for stolen vehicles. At regular intervals, officers report to police headquarters from call boxes, radios, or telephones.

Regardless of where they work, police, detectives, and special agents must write reports and maintain police records. They may be called to testify in court when their arrests result in legal action. Some officers, such as division or bureau chiefs, are responsible for training or certain kinds of criminal investigations, and those who command police operations in an assigned area have administrative and supervisory duties.

TRAINING

Civil service regulations govern the appointment of police and detectives in practically all states and large cities and in many small ones. Candidates must be U.S. citizens, be usually at least twenty years of age, and meet rigorous physical and personal qualifications. Eligibility for appointment depends on performance in competitive written examinations as well as on education and experience. Physical examinations often include tests of vision, strength, and agility.

Because personal characteristics such as honesty, good judgment, and a sense of responsibility are especially important in police and detective work, candidates are interviewed by a senior officer at police headquarters, and their character traits and background are investigated. In some police departments, candidates also may be interviewed by psychiatrists or psychologists or be given personality tests. Most applicants are subjected to lie detector examinations and drug testing. Some police departments subject police officers in sensitive positions to drug testing as a condition of continuing employment.

In large police departments, where most jobs are found, applicants usually must have high school educations. An increasing number of cities and states require some college training, and some hire law enforcement students as police interns; some departments require a college degree. A few police departments accept as recruits applicants who have less than high school educations, particularly if they have worked in fields related to law enforcement.

To be considered for appointment as an FBI special agent, an applicant must be a graduate of an accredited law school;

a college graduate with a major in accounting, engineering, or computer science; or a college graduate with either fluency in a foreign language or three years of full-time work experience. Applicants must be U.S. citizens, between twenty-three and thirty-five years of age at the time of appointment, and willing to accept an assignment anywhere in the United States. They also must be in excellent physical condition with at least 20/200 vision corrected to 20/40 in one eye and 20/20 in the other eye. All new agents undergo fifteen weeks of training at the FBI Academy at the U.S. Marine Corps base in Quantico, Virginia.

Applicants for special agent jobs with the U.S. Department of Treasury must have bachelor's degrees or a minimum of three years' work experience of which at least two are in criminal investigation. Candidates must be in excellent physical condition and be less than thirty-five years of age at the time they enter duty. Treasury agents undergo eight weeks of training at the Federal Law Enforcement Training Center in Glynco, Georgia, and another eight weeks of specialized training with their particular bureaus.

Applicants for special agent jobs with the U.S. Drug Enforcement Administration must have college degrees in any field and either one year of experience conducting criminal investigations or a record of college scholastic excellence. The minimum age for entry is twenty-one and the maximum age is thirty-six. Drug enforcement agents undergo fourteen weeks of specialized training at the FBI Academy in Quantico, Virginia.

More and more police departments are encouraging applicants to take post–high school training in law enforcement. Many entrants to police and detective jobs have completed some formal postsecondary education, and a significant number are college graduates. Many junior colleges, colleges, and universities offer programs in law enforcement or administration of justice. Other courses helpful in preparing for a police career include psychology, counseling, English, American history, public administration, public relations, sociology, business law, chemistry, and physics. Participation in physical education and sports is especially helpful in developing the stamina and agility needed for police work. Knowledge of a foreign language is an asset in areas that have concentrations of ethnic populations.

Some large cities hire high school graduates who are still in their teens as civilian police cadets or trainees. They do clerical work and attend classes and are appointed to the regular force at age twenty-one if qualified.

Before their first assignments, officers usually go through a period of training. In small communities, recruits work for a short time with experienced officers. In state and large city police departments, they get more formal training that may last a number of weeks or months. This training includes classroom instruction in constitutional law and civil rights, state laws and local ordinances, and accident investigation. Recruits also receive training and supervised experience in patrol, traffic control, use of firearms, self-defense, first aid, and handling emergencies.

Police officers usually become eligible for promotion after a probationary period ranging from six months to three years. In a large department, promotion may enable an officer to become a detective or specialize in one type of police work such as laboratory analysis of evidence, traffic control, communications, or working with juveniles. Promotion to sergeant, lieutenant, or captain usually is made according to a candidate's position on a promotion list, as determined by scores on a written examination and on-the-job performance.

Many types of training help police officers and detectives improve their job performance. Through training given at police department academies and colleges, required annually in many states, officers keep abreast of crowd-control techniques, civil defense, legal developments that affect their work, and advances in law enforcement equipment. Many police departments pay all or part of the tuition for officers to work toward associate and bachelor's degrees in law enforcement, police science, administration of justice, or public administration and pay higher salaries to those who earn degrees.

JOB OUTLOOK

Employment of police officers, detectives, and special agents is expected to increase more slowly than the average for all occupations through the year 2005. A more security-conscious society and growing concern about drug-related crimes should contribute to the increasing demand for police services. However, employment growth will be tempered somewhat by continuing budgetary constraints faced by law enforcement agencies. In addition, private security firms may increasingly assume some routine police duties such as crowd surveillance at airports and other public places. Although turnover in police, detective, and special agent jobs is among the lowest of all occupations, the need to replace workers who retire, transfer to other occupations, or stop working for other reasons will be the source of most job openings.

The opportunity for public service through police work is attractive to many. The job frequently is challenging and involves much responsibility. Furthermore, in many communities, police officers may retire with a pension to pursue second careers while still in their forties. Because of attractive salaries and benefits, the number of qualified candidates generally exceeds the number of job openings in many federal agencies and some state and local police departments, resulting in increased hiring standards and selectivity by employers. Competition is expected to remain keen for higher paying jobs in larger police departments. Persons having college training in law enforcement should have the best opportunities. Opportunities will be best in those communities whose departments are expanding and are having difficulty attracting an adequate supply of police officers.

Competition is expected to be extremely keen for special agent positions with the FBI, Department of Treasury, and Drug Enforcement Administration, as these prestigious jobs tend to attract a far greater number of applicants than the number of job openings. Consequently, only the most highly qualified candidates will obtain jobs.

The level of government spending influences the employment of police officers, detectives, and special agents. The number of job opportunities, therefore, can vary from year to year and from place to place. Layoffs, on the other hand, are rare because early retirements enable most staffing cuts to be handled through attrition. Police officers who lose their jobs from budget cuts usually have little difficulty finding jobs with other police departments.

SALARIES

In 1992, the median salary of nonsupervisory police officers and detectives was about $32,000 a year. The middle 50 percent earned between about $24,500 and $41,200; the lowest–paid 10 percent were paid less than $18,400, while the highest–paid 10 percent earned over $51,200 a year. Generally, salaries tend to be higher in larger, more urban jurisdictions that usually have bigger police departments.

Police officers and detectives in supervisory positions had in 1992 a median salary of about $38,100 a year. The middle 50 percent earned between about $28,300 and $49,800; the lowest–paid 10 percent were paid less than $23,200, while the highest–paid 10 percent earned over $58,400 annually.

Sheriffs, bailiffs, and other law enforcement officers had a median annual salary of about $25,800 in 1992. The middle 50 percent earned between about $20,500 and $30,900; the lowest–paid 10 percent were paid less than $15,600, while the highest–paid 10 percent earned over $38,800.

In 1993, FBI agents started at about $30,600 a year, while Department of Treasury agents started at about $18,300 or $22,700 a year and Drug Enforcement Agency agents at either $22,700 or $27,800 a year, depending on their qualifications. Salaries of experienced FBI agents started at around $47,900, while supervisory agents started at around $56,600 a year. Salaries of experienced Department of Treasury and Drug Enforcement Agency agents started at $40,200, while supervisory agents started at $47,900. Federal agents may be eligible for a special law enforcement compensation and retirement plan; applicants should ask their recruiters for more information.

Total earnings frequently exceed the stated salary due to payments for overtime, which can be significant, especially during criminal investigations or when police are needed for crowd control during sporting events or political rallies. In addition to offering the common fringe benefits (paid vacation, sick leave, and medical and life insurance), most police departments and federal agencies provide officers with special allowances for uniforms, and they furnish revolvers, nightsticks, handcuffs, and other required equipment. In addition, because police officers generally are covered by liberal pension plans, many retire at half-pay after twenty or twenty-five years of service.

RELATED FIELDS

Police officers maintain law and order in the nation's cities, towns, and rural areas. Workers in related law enforcement occupations include guards, bailiffs, correction officers, fire marshals, and fish and game wardens.

INTERVIEW
Rick Fitzgerald
Deputy Sheriff

Rick Fitzgerald is a deputy sheriff with the Broward County Sheriff's Office in South Florida. He has been doing police work since 1986.

What the Job Is Really Like

"Although the duties of the sheriff's office might differ from state to state, in Broward County we handle the jails, we handle all civil injunctions (evictions, serving restraining orders) we handle the unincorporated areas, and we also handle what we call contract cities. Some cities in the county, rather than hiring their own police department, discover they can save money by contracting with the sheriff directly. That happened to me. I worked for the City of Tamarac Police Department, and then one day I came in and found that the city had contracted with the sheriff's office to take over the police work. My job stayed the same; I just had to wear a different uniform.

"I work in road patrol, which is basically what your normal street police officer does. That involves answering calls, working traffic accidents, enforcing traffic laws, and writing tickets and stuff like that. Fortunately for me, I work in a quiet city.

"Probably one thing a lot of people fail to see, or don't know about until they get into this line of work, is the amount of paperwork a police officer does. A lot of paperwork is generated for all the different types of calls, and sometimes you find yourself writing up meaningless reports. People need reports to go to court or for an insurance claim, but these reports are for things that really aren't police matters. But we have to get involved because other concerns require these reports.

"I've handled just about anything you can imagine. I've taken all kinds of strange reports, all the way from something meaningless to a very serious call. Here's an example of what I mean by a meaningless call. A few months ago, a lady came in to tell me she lost her hearing aid. I told her that there were no serial numbers on hearing aids, that there was nothing we could trace or track to her. A police report is not warranted here; you don't need a police report. She didn't know that at the time, and she said "okay" and left. But lo and behold, she came back to me three weeks later and said, "Look, I do need you to make a report. I realize it's ridiculous, but my insurance company won't pay me the $400 for the hearing aid unless I give them a police report." Sometimes we end up feeling like glorified secretaries.

"Traffic accidents are another example. Minor traffic accidents where there are no criminal offenses shouldn't be a police matter. It's a civil matter to begin with and unless there's a crime involved—the driver's license had been suspended, or it's a DUI or there are any injuries—we shouldn't have to be involved. But the report we end up having to write is just for the insurance company. It can take up an hour of our time.

"I work eight–hour days, five on, two off. I spend all eight hours on the road, and so I have to do all the paperwork in my car on a clipboard. And you hope that you have time between your calls to get all the paperwork done. Today, for example, I was extremely busy and I just went from one call to another.

"During the course of the day, I went to a bank for two different forgeries—someone had stolen some checks and forged signatures. I also had a call for a runaway juvenile, so that right there made three reports that I had to try to write in between my other duties.

"In road patrol your job entails everything. They expect you to handle your calls; they expect you to write a few tickets. Your calls run the gamut. There are what we call *delayed calls*—a burglary, for example, that occurred a few hours before. Someone goes to bed at night and wakes up in the morning to discover his car has been broken into and the radio's gone.

"I work the day shift from 6:30 in the morning until 2:30. During that time period, we get a lot of delayed calls. The afternoon shift and midnight shift guys get a lot of what we call *in progress calls*. Someone gets up at 2:00 in the morning to go to the bathroom and looks out the window and sees a thief inside her car.

"But we get silly calls, too. Back when I was working the midnight shift I had someone call me up to tell me that their toilet was overflowing. They didn't know who to call so they called the police. I suggested a plumber, but meanwhile, we're obligated to go out there, and I reached behind the lady's toilet and shut off the water.

"These kinds of things get repetitive. You do them every day and it gets old. But I'm basically happy doing what I'm doing. I'm working a schedule that's very convenient for my wife and me to take care of our young daughter. I have no real desire to go up the ladder to sergeant, which is the next step. Although it's a raise in pay and status, I'd lose my seniority and have to go back to the midnight shift. Maybe later, once my daughter is in school, that could be an option.

"There are certain types of calls that I like. I do like working traffic accidents. That interests me. And what feels really nice is when someone gives you a hearty thank you for something you've done—if they've broken down alongside of the road and you stop and get them a tow truck, for example. They're extremely grateful for the help. And even better than that is when they write to the sheriff to say what a good job they feel you've done. That goes in your file and stays in your file."

How Rick Fitzgerald Got Started

"My father has been a policeman for about twenty-three years. I went to college and got my bachelor's degree in business from Florida International University. That was in 1985. At that time, a million people had business degrees, so I wondered what I would do. The opportunity to become a policeman was there, it had always been in the back of my mind, so I decided to pursue it. I went to City Hall and picked up an application. They hired me and put me through training. The police academy program took four months. I started getting a paycheck the minute I entered the academy. The irony was that I made more money during training than when I first came out to do police work. That was because you go to the police academy ten hours a day, fifty hours a week. You're getting ten hours of overtime each week. Once you graduate, you don't put in that kind of regular overtime, so your pay drops down."

Expert Advice

"My advice is probably the same thing my father told me: Just go in, do your eight hours and go home. Don't voice an opinion, don't get involved in the politics of the game, don't get involved in talking about people behind their back; it will just get you jammed up."

● ● ●

FOR MORE INFORMATION

Information about entrance requirements may be obtained from federal, state, and local civil service commissions or police departments.

Contact any Office of Personnel Management or Job Information Center for pamphlets providing general information and instructions for submitting an application for Treasury special agent, drug enforcement agent, FBI special agent, or U.S. marshal jobs. Look under U.S. Government, Office of Personnel Management in your telephone directory to obtain a local telephone number.

Information about law enforcement careers in general may be obtained from

International Union of Police Associations
1016 Duke Street
Alexandria, VA 22314

CHAPTER 4 Firefighting

EDUCATION
H.S. degree and other
training required

$$$ SALARY
$18,000–$100,000

OVERVIEW

Today's firefighters are brave and dedicated men and women who love the challenge and satisfaction of helping people in trouble. They risk their lives every day, saving victims trapped in burning buildings, pulling children out of wrecked cars, battling forest fires, or containing dangerous chemicals that have spilled and are threatening lives or the environment.

Firefighters are a special breed. They are go-getters, team players, and strong-minded individuals who know how to get a job done and done well.

Because most fire departments combine fire with rescue service, calls come in that can involve anything from car wrecks and heart attacks to kitchen fires or full warehouse blazes.

Firefighters have to be prepared to handle any type of call. They work odd hours, usually twenty-four hour shifts, with forty-eight or seventy-two hours off between. During that twenty-four-hour period, they are on call and can never really relax. The tones can start sounding at any time—in the middle of a meal, during a training session, or late at night when firefighters are fast asleep in the dorm.

Because of the emergencies and traumas these people share, firefighters feel very close to their coworkers. Most firefighters will tell you it's like being with a close-knit family, like brothers and sisters working together.

Although shift work can be grueling, there is a lot of time off between shifts. Firefighters put this time to good use, furthering their educations or working at second jobs. There are firefighters who are also lawyers, teachers, private investigators, funeral directors, swimming pool remodelers, and anything else in between.

Teamwork is the most important aspect of being a firefighter. This is not a job for loners. Lives depend on cooperation and trust. On a team, the nozzle man or woman can't put water on the fire unless the engineer makes it happen, and that doesn't happen unless the mechanic has done his or her job, and so on. Every person has a role to play.

TRAINING

Gone are the days when a kid fresh out of high school could walk in the door and say, "Here I am. How 'bout a job?" In the past, fire departments would take on people and train them. The pay was low then, and it was dangerous work, and not that many people wanted to become firefighters.

These days there is much more competition, and most fire departments expect people to have undergone training before even applying for a job.

Those serious about working as firefighters should get some training first. Twelve-week firefighter training programs are usually offered at community colleges. Another option is to study in a two-year program for an associate degree in fire science.

Once hired, firefighters continue their training, either on their own or through in-house classes. All skills have to be kept current, and there are many specialties to learn.

It is also wise to have good verbal and writing skills. Firefighters are often called on to speak in front of groups, and they must also know how to write reports. Math and chemistry are important, too, and those who want to climb the administrative ladder should also take business and management courses.

But academics are only one part of it. Firefighters must also have physical and emotional strength. They wear heavy gear and carry heavy equipment—and regularly come across upsetting situations. Being able to cope is a necessity.

To further enhance employability, it's a good idea to try to get some related experience first. Volunteer fire departments still make up a large percentage of our country's firefighting force. They usually will accept trainees who are still in school. The Boy Scouts of America also has a program to train future firefighters.

RANKS AND DIVISIONS

The firefighting service is run in quasimilitary fashion. There are rules and regulations to follow, uniforms, roll call, assigned duties, and a ranking system.

Here is a list of the different divisions found in a fire department:

Operations

Fire and Safety Inspection/Public Education

Fire Investigation

Emergency Medical Services

Training

Administration

No matter in which division a person's work, he or she will have a rank. The titles and sometimes the specific duties vary from department to department, but the general responsibilities are the same.

Combat Firefighter

This is the rank that everyone starts out with. Many are content to stay at this rank; others work toward promotion and continue to move up the ladder. Firefighters do just as their title implies—they fight fires. They might also learn specialties and deal with hazardous materials or medical emergencies.

Driver/Engineer

This person is responsible for getting the crew and equipment to the scene. He or she dispenses tools and makes sure there is a sufficient water supply.

Lieutenant

This is a first-level supervisory position. The lieutenant is responsible for the station during his or her shift, for seeing that it's run properly, for assigning duties, and for ensuring the welfare and safety of his or her crew.

Battalion Chief/Captain/Division Chief/Commander

Division chiefs command the following different departments:

- **Training**—responsible for maintaining continuing education units for both firefighters and EMS personnel

- **Resource management division/support services/ purchasing**—responsible for every item purchased, all the equipment, day-to-day supplies, and the maintenance of fire and rescue vehicles

- **Fire prevention/public education**—responsible for fire inspectors, all programs dealing with the public, and generating revenue through inspection fees the city charges

- **EMS**—responsible for all the emergency medical care given on the different shifts; division head monitors personnel, vacations and days off, and scheduling and must ensure that all the vehicles have the appropriate crew and paramedics

- **Operations**—responsible for all the firefighting shifts; division head has duties similar to those of EMS division head

In smaller departments with smaller budgets, the divisions are sometimes combined and a division head will be responsible for more than one area of operation.

Supervisor

Many departments also have supervisors who report directly to division heads. They might supervise the hour-by-hour activities of a shift and, driving in a specially marked car, follow the trucks out on calls.

Deputy Chief/Assistant Chief

Some cities or municipalities have only one deputy chief responsible for all the different divisions within the organization. Other cities have several assistants or deputies, each responsible for a different division.

In the absence of the fire chief, the deputy chief is ultimately responsible. He or she will take over the day-to-day command or will represent the department, attending meetings in the chief's place.

Fire Chief

The fire chief is in charge of the entire organization, which is countywide or citywide, with several fire stations located throughout the zone.

In a nutshell, the fire chief is ultimately responsible for everything. He or she works with whatever government body is responsible for fire and rescue functions, planning services and seeing that the plans are put into action. For example, a fire system might aim for a three-minute response time on paramedic calls and five minutes on fire calls. It's the fire chief's job to make sure that plan works. Basically, it's the chief's duty to manage the organization with its resources, personnel, and equipment, to meet those goals the city has established.

The chief is also expected to be the ultimate professional expert in the field. The fire chief can be appointed by a government official, but as is more and more common, he or she may have been a career firefighter who has gone through the ranks.

THE PATHS YOU CAN TAKE

Once on the force, the firefighter has a number of options, and he or she doesn't have to be promoted to driver/engineer or lieutenant to take advantage of them. To get on a specialist team, a firefighter first has to exhibit a desire to do the work. Then there has to be an opening on a particular team. But even more important, the team has to feel the person would make a good addition to its ranks. Members have to trust him or her and have confidence in his or her ability to learn.

In addition, each team requires certain training or skills. Here is a list of the different specialty teams a person can train for:

Extrication Specialist

These specialists know how to operate the jaws of life, a valuable tool for cutting out victims trapped in car wrecks.

Training is acquired in a number of ways. Those interested can take courses and seminars offered by rescue equipment manufacturers, learn on-the-job, or practice on junk cars on their own time. They have to be familiar with levers and hydraulics and understand automobile construction, knowing where both the weak and strong points are.

High-Angle Rescuer

These rescuers know how to use ropes and ladders and work at heights above two stories. They can rappel off tall buildings where ladders won't reach or climb up on water tanks or down dangerous cliffsides.

The specialized skills used in high-angle rescues are learned through local fire academies or community colleges and through on-the-job training. Obviously, potential high-angle team members cannot be afraid of heights. They must have steady nerves and, as all firefighters should, they should be in good physical condition.

Hazardous Materials Technician

This specialty is commonly known as *Haz-Mat*. Haz-Mat technicians are familiar with all sorts of chemicals and their containers. They also learn about valves and plumbing and patching. When there's an accident or a spill and these materials escape their sites and pose public risk, Haz-Mat firefighters step in.

Haz-Mat trainees study chemicals and their behavior if they are spilled or are involved in a fire. They learn how to use heat detectors and monitors. They also use computers to help in researching and identifying different chemicals. Programs are offered through fire academies and community colleges, and continuing education courses are given at individual fire departments. Because new chemicals are constantly turning up on the market, study is an ongoing process.

Technical Rescuer

This includes underground rescue in confined spaces. Urban search and rescue specialists are expert in finding people in the aftermath of hurricanes or earthquakes, when buildings have collapsed and trapped victims under piles of rubble. Technical rescuers also know how to pull out dogs or other animals trapped in wells or drain pipes.

Techniques for technical rescues are taught in fire academies and community college fire science programs and during in-house continuing education training.

Underwater Rescuer

Underwater rescue teams are trained to dive in the ocean, in lakes, and into dark canals. They know how to operate with zero visibility, feeling their way along the bottom with their hands, searching for submerged cars or bodies.

These experts are all trained as certified divers. They have to be expert swimmers first, with strength and endurance. In addition to having the skills every scuba diver learns, underwater rescue divers must know how to work in pitch black conditions, in freezing water, or in dangerous rapids or heavy surf conditions. They must also be familiar with equipment such as grappling hooks or inflatable boats.

Emergency Medical Technician

Emergency medical technicians and paramedics are versed in all sorts of medical emergencies. Their role and the training they receive are covered in depth in *On the Job: Real People Working in Health and Medicine*.

ADVANCEMENT

It is important for future administrators to develop good writing, speaking, and reading skills. In today's fire service, candidates for promotion take a civil service exam that tests writing skills, reading comprehension, and technical knowledge.

Verbal skills are also tested in an oral interview format, and specific administrative skills are assessed in role-playing activities. Candidates are judged on how they make tactical decisions in firefighting situations; how they perform with "in-basket/out-basket" exercises, handling administrative situations; and how they deal with personnel problems.

Ongoing employee evaluations and recommendations from supervisors also play a part in whether a candidate is promoted.

Many of the specific skills a candidate needs to move up the ladder can be developed on the job. Candidates for advancement should assist supervisors with their duties and take business and management courses when they are offered.

JOB OUTLOOK

The number of qualified applicants in most areas generally exceeds the number of job openings, even though the written examination and physical requirements eliminate many applicants. This situation is expected to persist through the year 2005.

Employment of firefighters is expected to increase about as fast as the average for all occupations through the year 2005 as a result of the increase in the nation's population and fire protection needs.

In addition, the number of paid firefighter positions is expected to increase as a percentage of all firefighter jobs. Much of the expected increase will occur in smaller communities with expanding populations that augment volunteers with career firefighters to better meet growing, increasingly complex fire protection needs. However, little growth is expected in large, urban fire departments. A small number of local governments are expected to contract for firefighting services with private companies.

Turnover of firefighter jobs is unusually low, particularly for an occupation that requires a relatively limited investment in formal education. Nevertheless, most job openings are expected to result from the need to replace those who retire or stop working for other reasons or who transfer to other occupations.

Layoffs of firefighters are not common. Fire protection is an essential service, and citizens are likely to exert considerable pressure on city officials to expand or at least preserve the level of fire protection coverage. Even when budget cuts do occur, local fire departments usually cut expenses by postponing equipment purchases or not hiring new firefighters rather than by laying off staff.

SALARIES

As with any profession, salaries vary depending upon the region of the country and the size of the department's budget. Generally speaking, firefighters can start anywhere from the high teens to $40,000 a year or more. At the highest levels, salaries are very attractive. Fire chiefs can earn between $85,000 and $100,000 a year and sometimes more. Raises come regularly and salaries increase with the special skills learned.

Some departments are able to reward firefighters with bonuses for years of service or give merit increases when they earn outstanding evaluations. The more degrees and certifications a firefighter has, the more money he or she will make.

RELATED FIELDS

A related firefighting occupation is the fire protection engineer, who identifies fire hazards in homes and workplaces and designs prevention programs and automatic fire detection and extinguishing systems. Other occupations in which workers respond to emergencies include police officers (see Chapter 3) and paramedics and emergency medical technicians (see the information earlier in this chapter and in *On the Job: Real People Working in Health and Medicine*).

INTERVIEW
Samantha Kievman
Firefighter

Samantha Kievman is a firefighter, an EMT, and a paramedic. She has been with her fire department since 1993.

What the Job Is Really Like

"In the fire service you see it all and you do it all. You get to meet so many people; you're always surrounded by people. When you pull up on scene, they're so happy to see you. It's great.

"We go on so many calls. All sorts of fires—cars, houses, kitchens. There are also medical calls—slip and falls or chest pains or car accidents. Anything you can imagine.

"The work is challenging, different. You never know what to expect. When you come into work you have to be on the alert for twenty-four hours. No matter what you're doing you have to stop to go on a call and you'll never know what it will be. The call could be for a simple slip and fall, but when you get there the guy is having chest pains. We could have a quiet day or a day where we're running twenty-four hours straight without stopping.

"When we're not out on a call, we have station duties. One day a week we take everything out of the kitchen, mop the floors, wipe down the walls, clean out the refrigerators, clean the stove; a lot more than I do at my own house. Then another day, we clean out the dorm, put up all the beds, wipe them down, vacuum. On Saturday it's lawn day; we do all our own lawn maintenance. And if something goes wrong at the station, we fix it. Every day there's something else to do.

"We also have training sessions. We watch training videos or have classes—Haz-Mat technician training, EMT refresher courses, paramedic meetings once a month.

"It's a great job, but there are some downsides. There's a lot of pressure when you pull up on a car accident and you've got four victims and they're all bad. You're running around and there are twenty people on scene and everyone's doing something.

"And if someone dies, it's terrible. Although we'd like to, we can't save everybody. You kind of have to make yourself cold to it. If you let it bother you, you can't do your job. You have to have compassion, but you also have to put up a little wall so you can handle the job and go back for your next twenty-four-hour shift."

How Samantha Kievman Got Started

"Before I even applied for a job, I went to a community college to become an EMT first. That took one semester. When I finished that, I attended a local fire training academy for another twelve weeks. When I started working as a firefighter, I also attended paramedic school.

"Training starts first thing in the morning and finishes up at six or so at night, five days a week for twelve weeks. Every morning you run a mile and a half, do sit-ups and pull-ups—all sorts of different workouts.

"Then you get cleaned up and go into the classroom and work with textbooks. We review something in class and then we go outside and actually do it. If it was a hose lay, we'd get bunkered out (put our gear on) and do a hose lay. If it was something to do with ladders, we'd go outside and get the ladders out.

"In a training facility they would smoke up a room. We'd put our air bottles on. There'd be flares set up to indicate where the fire was. We'd have to ladder the building and climb up to the second floor, bring up the hose line, open it up, and flow water. Everything is as realistic as possible.

"Not everyone makes it through the training program. Either they can't keep up physically or academically. I came home and studied every night. It's exhausting. You're climbing and lugging heavy dummies and equipment. It's physically and mentally demanding.

"When I took my state tests, the written and practical, I felt really confident. I had studied and put a lot of time into it."

Expert Advice

"Go for it! Go to EMT school, go to paramedic school, go through fire school, get as much schooling as you possibly can. Some fire departments won't even accept your application unless you're EMT and firefighting certified.

"The fire service wants someone who's going to put in 100 percent. We're dealing with people's lives. You don't want second best; you want top-notch people."

● ● ●

INTERVIEW
Jerry O'Brien
Driver/Engineer

Jerry O'Brien is a driver/engineer and also a Haz-Mat technician. He has been a firefighter since 1982 and has worked for two different fire departments on opposite ends of the country. He has taken the test for lieutenant and is number one on the list. He expects to get promoted this year.

What the Job Is Really Like

"You have to maintain the apparatus and equipment. You do a daily bumper-to-bumper inspection of every piece of equipment that's on board to make sure it's all in working order. All the medical gear has to be inspected; all the tools have to be in a state of readiness; there has to be oil, gas, and water in the truck; and you have to make sure the hose lines are correct.

"The next thing you are responsible for is transporting the firefighters and the crew to whatever assignment you've received. It could be a medical call or a fire or going to a train wreck. You could be driving in a lot of traffic.

"At a fire you are responsible for supplying water for the fire suppression—both establishing enough water coming into the engine from the hydrant and pumping it out to the structure.

"Once the water is flowing, the engineer has to make sure it doesn't fall off. If it did fall off, the firefighters' lives would be in extreme danger.

"You're also responsible for dispensing all of the tools on the apparatus, the axes, pry bars, whatever is needed.

"Or you might start up a generator and bring lights into the scene. The engineer is the one in the crew who's making all of the parts come together at the fire scene.

"The fun thing about being an engineer is getting to drive a big truck. I've driven fire engines in the mountains, on ice, on all kinds of terrain. And you're handling a million things at once. It's a challenge and at the fire you get a good feeling from everything running smoothly.

"The tough part is you don't get to go into the fire. It's hard to sit there and watch your buddies put on their air packs and go in to attack a fire. I was a firefighter before, and this job is a promotion, but it takes you out of the heat for a while. Literally. And you don't get back into that position until you get promoted again to lieutenant.

"A lot of us are in this because it's fun to put out a fire. It's like going into combat or playing football."

How Jerry O'Brien Got Started

"I didn't anticipate getting into the fire service; I stumbled upon it by accident. I was managing a retail store working seventy or eighty hours a week, killing myself. I saw an ad in the paper for the fire department. I went through the physical and written testing and then I got hired after about a year and a half on the waiting list. Once I got into the fire service, I found out that firefighters study a lot; they actually go to college and learn fire behavior, rescue techniques, high-angle rescue. I found it fascinating.

"To become an engineer in most fire departments you must have at least three years as a firefighter. During that time, you study books and manuals on water flow, the apparatus itself, and driving in hazardous conditions. You have to know your equipment.

"There's a written test and a practical test. You hook up to a hydrant and are given a couple of problems. For example, you're told to stretch an inch and three quarters hose and a two-and-a-half-inch hose and flow them at the correct water pressures. You have to be able to go to the pump panel and make split-second calculations and then operate the apparatus in such a way that doesn't overpressure a line. People will be on the end of that line.

"The practical portion of the exam is a real challenge. You need a knowledge of basic math and algebra and how to use hydraulic formulas. You have to know how to plug the numbers in. Some of the newer trucks actually will do a lot of the calculating for you and will have flow meters on the truck for you. Technology has simplified the job."

Expert Advice

"Education is crucial these days. You should think about earning a college degree—in EMS and fire science—because that's becoming more and more important. There aren't many bachelor's degree programs now—it's mainly at the associate's level—but in coming years there will be more and more four-year programs.

"And when opportunities present themselves to learn new skills, through your organization or on your own, take advantage of it. You need to grow and to learn more than your job."

●   ●   ●

INTERVIEW
Rob Brantley
Extrication Specialist

Rob Brantley has been a firefighter since 1975. In addition to being an extrication specialist, he is also an EMT and is a member of several other specialty teams.

What the Job Is Really Like

"I go out on fires—houses or cars or boats. You can't imagine the different things that can catch on fire. Warehouses are the most dangerous because you don't know what's inside. There could be gunpowder or chemicals.

"I also go out on any kind of auto accident. We'll get a Signal Four, which is an accident, usually with injuries. We go there to stabilize the situation, remove any danger to life or property. For example, if the car crashes into a house and the car is burning, we try to get the car out of the way so the house doesn't catch, too.

"I've seen some dreadful accidents. It bothers you, especially if you can't get someone out in time or it was too bad of a wreck and there was nothing you could do. And it can particularly bother you if it's a bad wreck with kids in it. It stays with me for a long time.

"We also do all kinds of medical and other kinds of rescues. But we don't often rescue cats from trees. If you think about it, you don't often see cat skeletons in trees—meaning they always manage to get themselves down.

"We've rescued quite a few pelicans out of trees, though. They get caught in fishing lines and then fly up into the trees and the line gets caught.

"We've also rescued dogs out of sewer pipes or gone out in the ocean for boat rescues. If a boat capsizes, we might get called before the Coast Guard, and that's when our dive team can go to work. We have a Zodiac, an inflatable boat, and a surf boat we can use to paddle out to the people.

"Working the jaws of life is my favorite thing to do. If someone is in trouble at a wreck, I like to feel I can get them out faster than anyone. I've spent a lot of time practicing taking cars apart."

How Rob Brantley Got Started

"I had always wanted to be a firefighter; in fact, no other job possibility had ever crossed my mind. In addition to my formal firefighting training, I went to some seminars, but most of my specialty training is from general knowledge. I worked with hydraulics before I got on the fire department. It's kind of a 'give me a lever, I can move the world' feeling. It seems to come naturally to me. It has to be in you. It's hard to force that stuff. If you want to get trained, most departments will train you.

"Everyone is exposed to all the different specialties, and if you want, you can go out of your way to practice. You can tell your supervisor you'd like to go over to the junkyard and practice taking cars apart.

"After the probation period, you can start investigating the teams in your department. But the crew has to have confidence in you. The person in charge of the team will take a poll—'Do you know such and such? What do you think? Could he or she do the job? Should we give them a try?'

"The teams are dangerous so you don't want someone next to you who's going to panic. Then you'll just have one more person to rescue."

Expert Advice

"To be an extrication specialist, you need common sense and you need to know about leverage and about how different parts of the cars will react to pressure—what will bend, what won't bend.

"There are parts of a car that are structurally less strong than others. You've got to know where and how to cut. You have to know how to take windshields out without getting glass all over everybody. Safety is the key. You don't want to hurt the person in the car any more than he's already been hurt; you don't want to hurt anybody that's standing around you.

"Also, there's a time factor. They call it the *Golden Hour*. Basically, you have an hour to get someone out of a wreck and to a trauma center to increase their chances of survival. You have to know how to act fast. You could make it worse if you pushed on the wrong part of the car; you could crush the person inside."

●   ●   ●

FOR MORE INFORMATION

The Boy Scouts of America has a great program for young people to learn about careers in firefighting. Through the Exploring Program, local fire departments will work with teens, provide them with uniforms, and teach them the basics of firefighting.

Once a week, they meet as a group with professional firefighters who are coordinating the program. They get general training in first aid, about the fire trucks, and about equipment. After they put in a certain number of hours and are tested, they are allowed to ride on the trucks. They are issued fire gear and can go to fires and other emergencies.

Although cadets are not allowed to go into burning buildings, the program is an excellent way to find out what it's really like to be a firefighter.

Cadets can start the program at age fourteen and stay in until they are twenty years old. Cadets often get hired as full-time firefighters right out of the program. The program is open to both girls and boys.

Boy Scouts of America
Exploring Program
P.O. Box 152079
Irving, TX 75015

International Association of Fire Fighters
1750 New York Avenue, NW
Washington, DC 20006

For additional information on salaries and hours of work for firefighters in various cities, consult the *Municipal Yearbook*, published by the International City Management Association. The yearbook is available in most libraries.

To get an idea about what firefighting exams are like, start practicing to get a head start and take a look at the following book at your library: *Arco Firefighter*, by Robert Andriuolo, Deputy Chief, New York City Fire Department, published by Prentice Hall.

This book helps prepare people for the different firefighter exams. It reviews all the subject matter a person needs to know, provides sample written and physical fitness tests, and gives tips and strategies for earning high test scores.

For information about professional qualifications and a list of two- and four-year degree programs in fire science or fire prevention, contact

National Fire Protection Association
Batterymarch Park
Quincy, MA 02269

For information about careers as a firefighter trainer, write to

The National Fire Academy
16825 South Seton Avenue
Emmitsburg, MD 21727

For information about administrative careers in firefighting, write to

International Association of Fire Chiefs
4025 Fair Ridge Drive
Fairfax, VA 22033

CHAPTER 5

The Internal Revenue Service

EDUCATION
B.A. and other training
   required

$$$ SALARY
$18,700–$84,500

OVERVIEW

Managers must have up-to-date financial information in order to make important decisions. Accountants and auditors prepare, analyze, and verify financial reports and taxes and monitor information systems that furnish this information to managers in all business, industrial, and government organizations.

The four major fields of accounting are government accounting, public accounting, management accounting, and internal auditing.

Government accountants and auditors maintain and examine the records of government agencies and audit private businesses and individuals whose activities are subject to government regulations or taxation. Specific information about working for the IRS is contained in the interview with Dawn Edwards, later in this chapter.

Public accountants have their own businesses or work for public accounting firms. They perform a broad range of accounting, auditing, tax, and consulting activities for their clients, who may be corporations, governments, nonprofit organizations, or individuals.

Management accountants (also called *industrial, corporate,* or *private accountants*) record and analyze the financial information of the companies for which they work.

Internal auditors verify the accuracy of their organization's records and check for mismanagement, waste, or fraud.

Within each field, accountants often concentrate on one phase of accounting. For example, many public accountants concentrate on tax matters, such as preparing individuals' income tax returns and advising companies of the tax advantages and disadvantages of certain business decisions.

Others concentrate on consulting and offer advice on matters such as employee health care benefits and compensation; the design of companies' accounting and data processing systems; and controls to safeguard assets.

Some specialize in forensic accounting investigating and interpreting bankruptcies and other complex financial transactions.

Still others work primarily in auditing, examining clients' financial statements and reporting to investors and authorities that they have been prepared and reported correctly. However, fewer accounting firms are performing this type of work because of potential liability.

Management accountants analyze and interpret the financial information corporate executives need to make sound business decisions. They also prepare financial reports for nonmanagement groups, including stockholders, creditors, regulatory agencies, and tax authorities. Within accounting departments, they may work in financial analysis, planning and budgeting, cost accounting, and other areas.

Accountants and auditors also work for federal, state, and local governments. Government accountants see that revenues are received and expenditures are made in accordance with laws and regulations. Many persons with accounting backgrounds work for the federal government as Internal Revenue Service agents or in financial management, financial institution examination, and budget analysis and administration.

Internal auditing is rapidly growing in importance. As computer systems make information more timely and available, top management can base its decisions on actual data rather than personal observation. Internal auditors examine and evaluate their firms' financial and information systems, management procedures, and internal controls to ensure that records are accurate and controls are adequate to protect against fraud and waste. They also review company operations, evaluating their efficiency, effectiveness, and compliance with corporate policies and procedures, laws, and government regulations. There are many types of highly specialized auditors, such as electronic data processing auditors, environmental auditors, engineering auditors, legal auditors, insurance premium auditors, bank auditors, and health care auditors.

In addition, a small number of persons trained as accountants teach and conduct research at business and professional schools. Some work part time as accountants or consultants.

Accountants and auditors work in offices, but public accountants may frequently visit the offices of clients while conducting audits. Self-employed accountants may be able to do part of their work at home. Accountants and auditors employed by large firms and government agencies may travel frequently to perform audits at clients' places of business, branches of their firms, or government facilities.

The majority of accountants and auditors generally work a standard forty-hour week, but many work longer, particularly if they are self-employed and free to take on the work of as many clients as they choose. For example, about four of ten self-employed accountants and auditors work more than fifty hours per week, compared to one of four wage and salary accountants and auditors. Tax specialists often work long hours during the tax season.

Computers are widely used in accounting and auditing. With the aid of special computer software packages, accountants summarize transactions in standard formats for financial records or organize data in special formats for financial analysis. These accounting packages are easily learned, require few specialized computer skills, and greatly reduce the amount of tedious manual work associated with figures and records.

Personal and laptop computers enable accountants and auditors in all fields, even those who work independently, to use their clients' computer systems and to extract information from large mainframe computers.

Internal auditors may recommend controls for their organizations' computer systems to ensure the reliability of the systems and the integrity of the data. A growing number of accountants and auditors have extensive computer skills and specialize in correcting problems with software or developing software to meet unique data needs.

TRAINING

Most public accounting and business firms require an applicant for an accountant or internal auditor position to have at least a bachelor's degree in accounting or a related field. Those wishing to pursue bachelor's degrees in accounting should carefully research accounting curricula before enrolling. Many states will soon require CPA candidates to complete 150 semester hours of coursework prior to taking the CPA exam, and many schools have altered their curricula accordingly.

Some employers prefer those with master's degrees in accounting or master's degrees in business administration with concentrations in accounting. Most employers also prefer applicants who are familiar with computers and their use in accounting and internal auditing.

For beginning accounting and auditing positions in the federal government, four years of college (including twenty-four semester hours in accounting or auditing) or an equivalent combination of education and experience are required.

Previous experience in accounting or auditing can help an applicant get a job. Many colleges offer students an opportunity to gain experience through summer or part-time internship programs conducted by public accounting or business firms. Such training is invaluable in gaining permanent employment in the field.

Professional recognition through certification or licensure also is helpful. In the majority of states, CPAs are the only accountants who are licensed and regulated. Anyone working as a CPA must have a certificate and a license issued by a state board of accountancy. The vast majority of states require CPA candidates to be college graduates, but a few states substitute a certain number of years of public accounting experience for the educational requirement.

Based on recommendations made by the American Institute of Certified Public Accountants and the National Association of State Boards of Accountancy, some states currently require that CPA candidates complete 150 semester hours of college coursework, and many other states are working toward adopting this law. This 150-hour rule requires an additional thirty hours of coursework beyond the usual four-year bachelor's degree in accounting.

All states use the four-part Uniform CPA Examination prepared by the American Institute of Certified Public Accountants. The two-day CPA examination is rigorous, and only about one-quarter of those who take it each year pass each part they attempt. Candidates are not required to pass all four parts at once, although most states require candidates to pass at least two parts for partial credit. Many states require all sections of the test to be passed within a certain period of time. Most states also require applicants for a CPA certificate to have some accounting experience.

The designations PA or RPA are also recognized by most states, and several states continue to issue these licenses. With the growth in the number of CPAs, however, the majority of states are phasing out the PA, RPA, and other non-CPA designations by not issuing any more new licenses. Accountants who hold PA or RPA designations have similar legal rights, duties, and obligations as CPAs, but their qualifications for licensure are less stringent.

The designation *accounting practitioner* is also awarded by several states. It requires less formal training than a CPA license and covers a more limited scope of practice.

Nearly all states require both CPAs and PAs to complete a certain number of hours of continuing professional education before their licenses can be renewed. The professional associations representing accountants sponsor numerous courses, seminars, group study programs, and other forms of continuing education.

Professional societies bestow other forms of credentials on a voluntary basis. Voluntary certification can attest to professional competence in a specialized field of accounting and auditing. It also can certify that a recognized level of professional competence has been achieved by accountants and auditors who acquired some skills on the job, without the amount of formal education or public accounting work experience needed to meet the rigorous standards required to take the CPA examination. Increasingly, employers seek applicants with these credentials.

The Institute of Internal Auditors confers the designation *Certified Internal Auditor* (CIA) upon graduates from accredited colleges and universities who have completed two years' work in internal auditing and who have passed a four-part examination.

The EDP Auditors Association confers the designation *Certified Information Systems Auditor* (CISA) upon candidates who pass an examination and who have five years of experience in auditing electronic data processing systems. However, auditing or data processing experience and college education may be substituted for up to three years.

Other organizations, such as the National Association of Certified Fraud Examiners and the Bank Administration Institute, confer different specialized auditing designations.

The Institute of Management Accountants (IMA), formerly the National Association of Accountants, confers the Certified Management Accountant (CMA) designation upon college graduates who pass a four-part examination, agree to meet continuing education requirements, comply with standards of professional conduct, and have at least two years' work in management accounting. The CMA program is administered through an affiliate of the IMA, the Institute of Certified Management Accountants. The Accreditation Council for Accountancy and Taxation, a satellite organization of the National Society of Public Accountants, awards a Certificate of Accreditation in Accountancy to those who pass a comprehensive examination and a Certificate of Accreditation in Taxation to those with appropriate experience and education. It is not uncommon for a practitioner to hold multiple licenses and designations. For instance, one internal auditor might be a CPA, CIA, and CISA.

Those planning careers in accounting should have an aptitude for mathematics; be able to analyze, compare, and interpret facts and figures quickly; and be able to make sound judgments based on this knowledge. They must be able to clearly communicate the results of their work, orally and in writing, to clients and management.

Accountants and auditors must be good at working with people as well as with business systems and computers. Accuracy and the ability to handle responsibility with limited supervision are important. Perhaps most important, because millions of financial statement users rely on their services, accountants and auditors should have high standards of integrity.

JOB OUTLOOK

Accountants and auditors held about 962,000 jobs in 1994. They worked in all types of firms and industries, but nearly one-third worked for accounting, auditing, and bookkeeping firms or were self-employed.

The majority of accountants and auditors were unlicensed management accountants, internal auditors, or government accountants and auditors. However, in 1994, there were on record over 500,000 state-licensed certified public accountants (CPAs), public accountants (PAs), registered public accountants (RPAs), and accounting practitioners (APs).

Most accountants and auditors work in urban areas where public accounting firms and central or regional offices of businesses are concentrated. Roughly 10 percent of all accountants are self-employed and less than 10 percent work part time.

Some accountants and auditors teach full time in junior colleges and colleges and universities; others teach part time while working for private industry or government or as self-employed accountants.

Employment of accountants and auditors is expected to grow faster than the average for all occupations through the year 2005. Qualified accountants and auditors should have good job opportunities. Although the profession is characterized by a relatively low rate of turnover, because the occupation is so large many openings also will arise as accountants and auditors retire, die, or move into other occupations.

CPAs should have the widest range of opportunities, especially as more states enact the 150-hour rule (see the preceding section, "Training") and it becomes more difficult to become a CPA.

As the economy grows, the number of business establishments increases, requiring more accountants and auditors to set up their books, prepare their taxes, and provide management advice. As these businesses grow, the volume and complexity of information developed by accountants and auditors on costs, expenditures, and taxes will increase as well.

More complex requirements for accountants and auditors also arise from changes in legislation related to taxes, financial reporting standards, business investments, mergers, and other financial matters.

The changing role of public accountants, management accountants, and internal auditors also will spur job growth. Public accountants will perform less auditing work due to potential liability and less tax work due to growing competition from tax preparation firms, but they will assume an even greater management advisory role and expand their consulting services. These rapidly growing services will lead to increased demand for public accountants in the coming years.

Management accountants also will take on greater advisory roles as they develop more sophisticated and flexible accounting systems and focus more on analyzing operations rather than on just providing financial data. Similarly, management will increasingly need internal auditors to develop new ways to discover and eliminate waste and fraud.

Despite growing opportunities for qualified accountants and auditors, competition for the most prestigious jobs, such as those with major accounting and business firms, will remain keen. Applicants with master's degrees in accounting, master's degrees in business administration with concentrations in accounting, or broad-based computer experience will have an advantage.

Moreover, computers now perform many simple accounting functions, allowing accountants and auditors to incorporate and analyze more information. This increasingly complex work requires greater knowledge of more specialized areas, such as international business and current legislation, and expertise in specific industries.

SALARIES

In the federal government, the starting annual salary for junior accountants and auditors was about $18,700 in 1995. Candidates who had a superior academic record could begin at about $23,000. Applicants with master's degrees or two years' professional experience began at $28,300.

Accountants employed by the federal government in non-supervisory, supervisory, and managerial positions averaged $50,500 and auditors $53,600 a year in 1995.

According to a National Association of Colleges and Employers survey in 1995, bachelor's degree candidates in accounting received starting salary offers averaging nearly $28,000 a year; master's degree candidates in accounting averaged $31,500.

According to another survey—of workplaces in 160 metropolitan areas—the most experienced accountants had median earnings of $77,200.

According to a survey conducted by Robert Half International, salaries of internal auditors in 1995 ranged from $23,000 for those with less than two years of experience to $84,500 for those with over ten years of experience.

RELATED FIELDS

Accountants and auditors design internal control systems and analyze financial data. Others for whom training in accounting is invaluable are appraisers, budget officers, loan officers, financial analysts and managers, bank officers, actuaries, underwriters, tax collectors and revenue agents, FBI special agents, securities sales workers, and purchasing agents.

INTERVIEW
Dawn Edwards
Internal Revenue Service Agent

In 1977, Dawn Edwards earned her B.A. in French and Spanish with a minor in Italian from Santa Clara University in California. She began working for the IRS in 1982.

What the Job Is Really Like

"I work for the Internal Revenue Service, Examination Division, in Miami, Florida. The IRS is an agency of the

Department of Treasury of the United States. Of course, it is a nationwide organization. Our national office is located in Washington, D.C.

"Under the national office are the regional offices, each of which covers several states. (At the present time, I am not sure how many district offices exist because the IRS just underwent a reorganization and I don't have all of the specifics.) These offices are the main offices that oversee the various district offices located in each state. The number of district offices in each state differs depending on the population and the need of service to the population. For example, the state of Florida is under the Atlanta Regional Office, which has two district offices: the Jacksonville District and the South Florida District (although these names may have changed during the reorganization of the IRS).

"Each district office is divided into many divisions, such as the Examination Division, the Collections Division, and the Criminal Investigation Division. Each division is then divided into branches, and each branch is made up of several groups. The group is the basic unit of the branch where the revenue agents, collections officers, or CID agents belong. For example, I am in the South Florida District, Examination Division, Branch Four, Group 1424.

"The IRS has many posts of duty (offices) throughout the states. In these posts of duty you can find branches and groups. For example, the South Florida District has several posts of duty including Miami, South Dade, North Dade, Plantation (this is also where the South Florida District is located), Sunrise, Fort Myers, Fort Pierce, Sarasota, West Palm Beach, and others.

"Although we have offices, the IRS allows its field employees (field employees are revenue agents, collections officers, CID agents, and anyone whose job requires that they go out of their offices in order to perform their duties) to work out of their homes, if the employee so chooses. However, most field employees are expected to work in the field at least 50 to 80 percent of their time. Since I am a revenue agent and my main duties are to audit corporations and partnerships, most of my time should be spent doing the examinations at the places of business or at the offices of the accountants that represent these entities.

"An audit of a return, be it a return of an individual or an entity, is not just auditing the books and records of the person. An audit includes reviewing the financial status or economic reality of the person or entity. This means that the examiner (agent) must evaluate the facts and circumstances of each case to determine if what is reported on the return is credible or not. For example, if a company has been reporting losses for a few years, we wonder how the company manages to survive. Are there related entities that loan moneys to this company? Do the shareholders contribute more capital? Do they get loans from financial institutions? If the answers to those questions are negative, then it is questionable that the company is in fact incurring losses every year.

"I have several duties.

"**Planning of Work.** I establish workload priorities for assigned cases, compliance activities (*compliance* means to ensure that all entities and people related to the cases I am assigned are in compliance with the tax laws—i.e., have filed tax returns), and other assignments such as planning, scheduling, and spending time on work-based priorities; planning the examinations, scheduling appointments required to conduct the examinations, and conducting examinations.

"**Application of Accounting and Auditing Principles.** I must gain an understanding of the taxpayer's accounting practices and bookkeeping systems. I have to reconcile amounts on the returns to the books and records and analyze the relationship between the income statements and the balance sheets accounts in order to identify potential issues. I must also determine the quality of the internal control of the company through interviews with the people involved in the business, employees, and/or accountants. After assessing the control structure, I select the audit techniques to use.

"**Issue Identification.** I review the returns and internal control of the companies to determine which are the significant items that may have tax potential.

"**Fact Finding.** I gather adequate evidence to resolve the tax issues identified and support the conclusions reached. And I evaluate the credibility of all evidence obtained.

"**Application of Tax Law.** I conduct necessary research to understand and clarify the tax law applicable to the case issues and facts. I apply the Internal Revenue Code, regulations, rulings, court cases, etc., to the case facts to decide issues and arrive at the correct tax determination.

"**Written Product.** I prepare workpapers that reflect the audit steps I've taken and that support the conclusions I've reached. I prepare accurate examination reports, schedules, and forms. And then I assemble the case file in order to close the case.

"**Customer Relations.** I conduct contacts and discussions both inside and outside the IRS in a professional manner.

"**Use of Time.** I try to consistently complete tasks so that the total time I spend is relatively low, and the time span of activities is relatively short, considering the nature and complexity of the work.

"There are really no typical days, per se. All of my cases are different. I usually have fifteen to twenty cases on my inventory.

"When I get a newly assigned case, I look at the return to determine issues. This means that I evaluate the return and the information in it to determine if any items should be checked in detail. I also look for related entities and people in order to do a compliance check (ensure that they have filed tax returns). I also ensure that the company itself has filed all required returns such as income tax returns for various years, employment tax returns, excise tax returns, state tax returns, and any other type of return. I then send a letter explaining the examination process, appeals rights, and representation rights, and then I make an appointment to start the examination. With the letter, I send a document request, detailing the books and records I need in order to conduct the examination.

"Between the time I send the letter and the time set to start the audit, different things may happen—some of which are

(a) getting a call from the owner of the company or the controller of the company to ask me questions about the audit and/or to postpone the appointment (most people want to postpone the appointment although I usually give them a month to prepare for the audit);

(b) getting a call from an accountant advising me he or she is representing the taxpayer (the accountant may also request a postponement of the audit and/or that the examination be moved to his or her office); or

(c) I don't hear anything from anyone so I call the owner of the company a week or so after sending the letter.

"Although I have the authority to set the date and place of the examination, I usually accommodate the requests of the taxpayer or the representative. However, I am required to conduct a tour of the business to familiarize myself with the surroundings and the business activities, so I always ensure this is understood and agreed upon by all parties involved.

"Once an agreement is reached as to the date and place of the audit, I go to the place of business on the date set to conduct the tour and hopefully interview the owner or one of the people in charge of the business. Then I start the examination of the books and records (whether at the place of business or at the accountant's office) to determine if everything has been properly treated on the return. I usually tie in all amounts to the books but only do an in-depth review of items that do not seem to be treated correctly.

"I conduct tax research to determine if the taxpayer is properly treating these items. If I find that everything is correctly treated on the return, the case is closed as is (called a *no-change case*). If I find that some item or items are incorrectly treated, I discuss them with the accountant and with the owner (if the latter wants to be present). If they can provide further explanations, court cases, rulings, etc., that I have not yet considered, then I study those to determine if they are right or not.

"If I find that they are right, the case is closed no-change. If I find that they are wrong, I advise them of my determination and request that they agree to it. The taxpayer has the right to agree or not agree. If the taxpayer agrees, I prepare a report proposing the changes and the additional tax due. The taxpayer or the representative signs the report to show agreement. I sign the report as the representative of the IRS. The case is then closed 'agreed' and the tax is assessed. Taxpayers may also be penalized for certain types of mistakes made, but the penalties are usually up to the discretion of the revenue agent. Interest is always assessed on any additional tax due.

"If the taxpayer does not agree with the adjustments proposed and the additional tax due, the case is closed 'unagreed.' I must then prepare a report outlining all of the adjustments proposed and the tax due. Attached to this report is a complete write-up of the facts, findings, audit steps taken, applicable tax law, and conclusions reached for each adjustment proposed.

"At times, when taxpayers receive this full report, they will change their mind and agree to the adjustments. If not, the case goes to the appeals division and possibly to tax court.

"My job is at times very interesting and at times very boring. It is definitely stressful. The interesting part for me is the fact that I meet so many different people with so many different ideas and ways of doing business. The boring part is looking at books and records all day long.

"In addition, I get bored working alone in places where I am not wanted and where people are wary of the IRS and the person who is representing this entity. I also get bored and tired of listening to the same lame excuses some of them give me for certain things. For example, I always catch them at their worst time or when they are the busiest or when they have an emergency business trip or when they just happen to have lost the records for the year I am auditing or when someone died in the family and they don't really need me to bother them on top of all of their other problems. After fifteen years of listening to these statements, I have had enough.

"The stressful part of this job comes from both inside and outside the IRS. The agency expects me to do a quality job in a minimum amount of time. Of course, it also expects me to find mistakes and get additional taxes paid (although they will never admit to this). Outside the IRS, I have to constantly deal with people who do not want to deal with me. I sometimes meet very nice people, sometimes not so nice, and sometimes downright nasty and mean, but none of them want me there!

"And, in spite of that, I have to get their cooperation during the examination, and I have to try to convince them that I am right when I find an adjustment and propose additional taxes. (Who wants to pay more taxes, anyway?)

"Besides doing audits, I may at times do other assigned jobs or jobs for which I volunteer—for example, on-the-job instructor, acting for a group manager, classifying returns (determining if the returns sent from the Service Center in Atlanta to the South Florida District warrant examination or not), and various other assignments.

"What I like most about my job is the security. By this I mean that I do not fear losing the job at any given time. I also like the flexibility with time, leave, and workplace.

"I will expand a bit on this.

"**Flexibility with Time.** The IRS allows its employees to start work at any time between 7:00 and 9:00 A.M. and finish the day any time between 3:30 and 5:30 P.M. It also allows the employees to work part time or accumulate hours (work extra hours in order to use them when you need them). In addition, I do not have to take work home if I do not finish what I planned to do on a specific day; this means that I work my eight hours a day and the rest of the time is mine (contrary to accountants who work for private firms and who, at times, have to work overtime whether they want to or not).

"**Flexibility with Leave.** Government employees accumulate a certain number of vacation and sick hours every pay period (each pay period is two weeks). As long as we have leave accumulated, we can take the hours any time we need them and in any increments (the lowest increment is one hour).

"**Flexibility of Workplace.** I am allowed to work from my house instead of the IRS office. I only go to the office when I have a meeting, to do monthly reports, to pick up mail, to get cases, to submit cases, and to do research. I can plan my work well enough ahead to try to get all office work done (except for meetings since I cannot control these) in one or two days a month.

"I don't like several things about my job. First, although I have a tremendous responsibility, 'management' treats me (and all other employees) as kids who have to be checked constantly to see if they are behaving. I do not like this lack of trust at all. Second, I do not like the fact that I am always in an uncomfortable situation—dealing with people who do not want anything to do with the IRS."

How Dawn Edwards Got Started

"I was never really attracted to this profession. I got into it by chance. I moved to Miami from California after I graduated, hoping to find a job in my field (languages). However, it become painfully clear that these jobs were not easily found. I found a job as a secretary in Immigration in 1978. Soon after that, I got a job as a secretary for the Equal Employment Office of the Coast Guard. Subsequently, I got a job as a secretary in the IRS. My boss and coworkers encouraged me to take accounting and business law courses in order to qualify for the revenue agent position.

"In order to get a secretarial job with any governmental agency, a person is required to pass a civil service entrance examination. Once I passed this examination, I went to the personnel department of each agency and applied for available positions.

"Since one of the qualifications of a revenue agent is to have a certain number of accounting and business law credits, I took the required credits in these subjects at Miami-Dade Community College in Miami, Florida. It took me about two years to get all of the required courses because I was working full time and studying part time.

"After completing the required accounting and business law courses, I applied for the revenue agent position, passed an interview, and got the job.

"In addition, once a person is hired as an Internal Revenue Agent, the IRS trains the new employee. The training consists of five phases and each phase is divided into two types of training: classroom and on the job.

"During the classroom training, the agent learns tax law and must take and pass tests.

"During the on-the-job training, the new agent conducts examinations under the guidance of an on-the-job instructor, who is usually an experienced agent. The total amount of time to complete these phases is about two to three years.

"The first year working for the IRS is conditional. This means that, if the agent does not pass the first couple of phases of training, he or she may be fired. After the first year, if the agent has passed all training during that year, the job becomes a career job or a permanent job."

Expert Advice

"You need to be aware that you are going to work for a bureaucratic entity where the red tape is endless and where you will not advance as quickly as you may wish. You also need to make sure you want to represent an entity that is disliked by most (if not all).

"In addition, you have to be prepared to hear all sorts of innuendos against yourself, but which are really against the IRS—you cannot take anything as a personal affront or you will not survive.

"You have to make sure you can deal with all sorts of people of every possible class, background, and education. Most of all, you have to learn to take it as easily as possible and not let the stress of the job ruin your personal life."

● ● ●

FOR MORE INFORMATION

Information about different accounting licenses and the standards for licensure in a state may be obtained from the state board of accountancy. A list of the addresses and chief executives of all state boards of accountancy is available from

> National Association of State Boards of Accountancy
> 380 Lexington Avenue, Suite 200
> New York, NY 10168-0002

Information about careers in certified public accounting and about CPA standards and examinations may be obtained from

> American Institute of Certified Public Accountants
> 1211 Avenue of the Americas
> New York, NY 10036-8775

Information on management and other specialized fields of accounting and auditing and on the Certified Management Accountant program is available from

> Institute of Management Accountants
> 10 Paragon Drive
> Montvale, NJ 07645-1760

> National Society of Public Accountants and the
> Accreditation Council for Accountancy and Taxation
> 1010 North Fairfax Street
> Alexandria, VA 22314

The Institute of Internal Auditors
249 Maitland Avenue
Altamonte Springs, FL 32701-4201

The EDP Auditors Association
455 Kehoe Boulevard, Suite 106
Carol Stream, IL 60188-0180

For information on accredited accounting programs and educational institutions offering specializations in accounting or business management, contact

American Assembly of Collegiate Schools of Business
605 Old Ballas Road, Suite 220
St. Louis, MO 63141

Contact the local IRS agency for hiring procedures.

CHAPTER 6 Postal Workers

🎓 EDUCATION
H.S. degree recommended;
other training required

$$$ SALARY
$24,000–$35,000

OVERVIEW

Each day, the U.S. Postal Service receives, sorts, and delivers millions of letters, bills, advertisements, and packages. To do this, it employs about 792,000 workers. Almost five out of ten of these workers are postal clerks, who sort mail and serve customers in post offices, or mail carriers, who deliver the mail.

Clerks and carriers are distinguished by the type of work they do. Clerks are usually classified by the mail processing function they perform, whereas carriers are classified according to their type of route—city or rural.

Postal Clerks

About 350 mail processing centers throughout the country service post offices in surrounding areas and are staffed primarily by postal clerks. Some clerks, more commonly referred to as *mail handlers*, unload the sacks of incoming mail; separate letters, parcel post, magazines, and newspapers; and transport these to the proper sorting and processing areas. In addition, they may load mail into automated letter-sorting machines, perform simple canceling operations, and rewrap packages damaged in processing.

After letters have been put through stamp-canceling machines, they are taken to other workrooms to be sorted according to destination. Clerks operating older electronic letter-sorting machines push keys corresponding to the zip codes of the local post offices to which each letter will be delivered; the machine then drops the letters into the proper slots. This older, less automated method of letter sorting is being slowly phased out.

Other clerks sort odd-sized letters, magazines, and newspapers by hand. Finally, the mail is sent to local post offices for sorting according to delivery route, and it's delivered.

A growing proportion of clerks operate optical character readers (OCRs) and bar code sorters. Optical character readers read the zip code and spray a bar code onto the mail. Bar code sorters then scan the code and sort the mail. Because this is significantly faster than older sorting methods, it is becoming the standard sorting technology in mail processing centers.

Postal clerks at local post offices sort local mail for delivery to individual customers; sell stamps, money orders, postal stationary, and mailing envelopes and boxes; weigh packages to determine postage; and check that packages are in satisfactory condition for mailing. Clerks also register, certify, and insure mail and answer questions about postage rates, post office boxes, mailing restrictions, and other postal matters. Occasionally, they may help customers file claims for damaged packages.

Mail Carriers

Once the mail has been processed and sorted, it is ready to be delivered by mail carriers. The duties of city and rural carriers are very similar. Most carriers travel established routes, delivering and collecting mail. Mail carriers start work at the post office early in the morning, where they spend a few hours arranging their mail for delivery and taking care of other details. Now, automated equipment is able to sort most of the mail for city carriers, allowing them to spend less time sorting and more time delivering mail.

Carriers may cover their routes on foot, by vehicle, or through a combination of both. On foot, they carry heavy loads of mail in satchels or push it in carts. In some urban and most rural areas, they use cars or small trucks. Although the Postal Service provides vehicles to city carriers, most rural carriers use their own automobiles. Deliveries are made house-to-house, to roadside mailboxes, and to large buildings, such as offices or apartments, which generally have all their mailboxes on the first floor.

Besides delivering and collecting mail, carriers collect money for postage due and C.O.D. (cash on delivery) fees and obtain signed receipts for registered, certified, and insured mail. If a customer is not home, the carrier leaves a notice that tells where special mail is being held.

After completing their routes, carriers return to the post office with mail gathered from street collection boxes, homes, and businesses. They turn in the mail receipts and money collected during the day and may separate letters and parcels for further processing by clerks.

The duties of some city carriers may be very specialized; some deliver only parcel post while others collect mail from street boxes and receiving boxes in office buildings. In contrast, rural carriers provide a wide range of postal services. In addition to delivering and picking up mail, they sell stamps and money orders and accept parcels, letters, and items to be registered, certified, or insured.

All carriers answer customers' questions about postal regulations and services and provide change-of-address cards and other postal forms when requested. In addition to carrying out their regularly scheduled duties, carriers often participate in neighborhood service programs in which they check on elderly or shut-in patrons or notify the police of any suspicious activities along their routes.

TRAINING

Postal clerks and mail carriers must be U.S. citizens or have been granted permanent resident-alien status in the United States. They must be at least eighteen years old (or sixteen, with a high school diploma). Qualification is based on a written examination that measures speed and accuracy at checking names and numbers and ability to memorize mail distribution procedures. Applicants must pass a physical examination as well and may be asked to show that they can lift and handle mail sacks weighing up to seventy pounds.

Applicants for jobs as postal clerks operating electronic sorting machines must pass a special examination that includes a machine aptitude test. Applicants for mail carrier positions must have drivers' licenses, good driving records, and passing grades on a road test.

Applicants should apply at the post office or mail processing center where they wish to work in order to determine when an exam will be given. Applicants' names are listed in order of their examination scores. Five points are added to the score of an honorably discharged veteran and ten points to the score of a veteran wounded in combat or disabled.

When a vacancy occurs, the appointing officer chooses one of the top three applicants; the rest of the names remain on the list to be considered for future openings until their eligibility expires, usually two years from the examination date.

Relatively few people under the age of twenty-five are hired as career postal clerks or mail carriers, a result of keen competition for these jobs and the customary waiting period of one to two years or more after passing the examination. It is not surprising, therefore, that most entrants transfer from other occupations.

New postal clerks and mail carriers are trained on the job by experienced workers. Many post offices offer classroom instruction. Workers receive additional instruction when new equipment or procedures are introduced. They usually are trained by other postal employees or sometimes by training specialists hired under contract by the Postal Service.

JOB OUTLOOK

Those seeking jobs in the Postal Service can expect to encounter keen competition as the number of applicants for postal clerk and mail carrier positions is expected to continue to far exceed the number of openings. Job opportunities will vary by occupation and duties performed.

Overall employment of postal clerks is expected to decline through the year 2005. In spite of anticipated increases in the total volume of mail, automation will continue to increase the productivity of postal clerks, slowing employment growth.

Increasingly, mail will be moved using automated materials-handling equipment and sorted using optical character readers, bar code sorters, and other automated sorting equipment. In addition, demand for window clerks will be moderated by the increased sales of stamps and other postal products by grocery and department stores and other retail outlets.

Jobs will become available because of the need to replace postal clerks and mail carriers who retire or stop working for other reasons. However, the factors that make entry to these occupations highly competitive—attractive salaries, a good pension plan, job security, and modest educational requirements—contribute to a high degree of job attachment. Accordingly, replacement needs produce relatively fewer job openings than do those of other occupations of this size. In contrast to the typical pattern, postal workers generally remain in their jobs until they retire; relatively few transfer to other occupations.

Although the volume of mail to be processed and delivered rises and falls with the level of business activity as well as with the season of the year, full-time postal clerks and mail carriers have never been laid off. When mail volume is high, full-time clerks and carriers work overtime, part-time clerks and carriers work additional hours, and casual clerks and carriers may be hired. When mail volume is low, overtime is curtailed, part-timers work fewer hours, and casual workers are discharged.

SALARIES

In 1992, base pay for beginning full-time carriers and postal clerks was $23,737 a year, rising to a maximum of $33,952 after twelve and one-half years of service. To those working between 6:00 P.M. and 6:00 A.M. a supplement is paid. Experienced, full-time, city delivery mail carriers earn an average salary of $32,832 a year.

Postal clerks and carriers working part-time, flexible schedules begin at $11.81 an hour and, based on the number of years of service, increase to a maximum of $16.91 an hour.

Rural delivery carriers had average base salaries of $34,951 in 1992. Their earnings are determined through an evaluation of the amount of work required to service their routes. Carriers with heavier workloads generally earn more than those with lighter workloads. Rural carriers also receive an equipment maintenance allowance when required to use their own vehicles. In 1992, this was approximately thirty-four cents per mile.

Postal workers enjoy a variety of employer-provided benefits. These include health and life insurance, vacation and sick leave, and a pension plan.

In addition to receiving their hourly wage and benefits package, some postal workers receive uniform allowances. These postal workers include those who are in the public view for four or more hours each day and various maintenance workers. The amount of the allowance depends on the job performed; some workers are only required to wear a partial uniform, and their allowance is lower. In 1992, for example, the allowance for a letter carrier was $252 per year, compared to $108 for a window clerk.

Most of these workers belong to one of four unions: American Postal Workers Union, National Association of Letter Carriers, National Postal Mail Handlers Union, and National Rural Letter Carriers Association.

RELATED FIELDS

Other workers whose duties are related to those of window clerks are mail clerks, file clerks, routing clerks, sorters, material-moving equipment operators, clerk typists, cashiers, data entry operators, and ticket sellers.

Others with duties related to those of mail carriers are messengers, merchandise deliverers, and delivery-route truck drivers.

INTERVIEW
Elsa Riehl
Window Clerk

Elsa Riehl has been with the Postal Service since 1975. She started in Houston as a letter-sorting machine (LSM) operator, sorting mail at night. She's worked as a subclerk, unloading and loading trucks and sorting the mail for the carriers, and has been a window clerk since 1993.

What the Job Is Really Like

"I'm responsible for selling stamps, taking in packages, helping customers over the window. I also sort mail for the post office boxes and I do special sortings for the large companies who pay an extra fee to have their mail handled early in the day. Early in the morning I also transport incoming mail from another station to our office.

"I like working with the public. Most of them are pretty easygoing and understanding. I like talking to people and helping them, letting them know what their options are regarding mailing. A lot of people are not aware of the different charges. I've seen in other post offices that a lot of clerks don't explain the services we offer to the customers. I like to be able to explain what priority mail is, what express mail is.

"I supervised for a while in Texas and I didn't care for it—I like working with people, I don't like giving the orders. Basically, I like my hours, I like the work itself. I work 6:30 A.M. to 3:30 P.M., Monday through Friday. A lot of times I come in early and stay late. And I get overtime for that. Anything over eight hours is overtime.

"There's job security, our pensions are good, our salary and benefits are excellent. We can't complain about that, and once we're in, it's very hard to get fired. We're protected through the union.

"But there's a lot of pressure and a lot of downsides working for the post office. For example, as window clerks we're responsible for all the stamps we sell. We carry anywhere from $15,000 to $30,000 or $40,000 in stock. We get audited every four months—unless there's a special situation (if a customer complains they were shortchanged, for example). Then we can request a special audit to protect ourselves. We won't open our window the next morning and the auditors will count every single stamp and every penny. If we don't ask for the special audit, we would have to make up the loss at the four-month audit. We're only given a $40 leeway. And that's not enough for four months and the amount of money we handle. Above that, it would come out of our pockets.

"Another problem is that we have no one to answer the phone, to handle customers that call in. Our managers want us, as window clerks, to walk away from our window and answer the phone. That's very hard to do if you're with a customer and you haven't collected the money yet, but you've given them the stamps. According to our supervisors, the customer is always right, but what do you do if you come back from the phone and say, 'Well, Ma'am, you haven't paid me,' and the customer says, 'Yes, I did.'"? Other stations have people to answer the phone and take care of complaints. We're a small office and we don't have that extra staff. The supervisors don't make it easy for us.

"It's not an easy atmosphere. If our upper managers don't get any better and if they don't get someone in there who knows more about window service and delivery, I think in a few years, the way it's going, everyone is talking about privatization. It's getting to the point where they're giving us supervisors who have no idea what our jobs are. A lot of the people who get promoted . . . well, it's not what they know, it's who they know.

"There are problems all throughout the Postal Service. If you do get a good manager, they tend to move up and out and someone else will come in.

"We're always shorthanded. They're aware of the problem. They preach customer service to us, but only when it's convenient for the managers.

"We do occasionally get nasty and arrogant customers, sometimes because we're understaffed. The managers always say to call them and they'll take care of it, but half the time you can't get them over to your station, you can't get them to talk to the customer, and you'll never get them to tell the customer we're short-staffed because they don't want to pay the extra overtime to make sure we're staffed properly.

"If you decide to transfer, you can lose your seniority. That happened to me when I left Texas and moved to Florida. You keep your years in service and the amount of vacation time you've accrued and retirement benefits, but when I transferred I had fifteen years in service, but people who had only three were over me in terms of vacation choices and other privileges."

How Elsa Riehl Got Started

"My brother-in-law had worked for the post office, had been with them for years. I was attending college, studying law enforcement, and looking for part-time work during the upcoming summer break. My brother-in-law suggested I take the postal exam. I took it in April of 1975 and was later told I scored 100 percent, which was very unusual. In June I was called for an interview. This was in Houston, Texas. A hurricane was on its way and I drove to the interview with my mother. We were pretty well under water, but I couldn't miss my interview. I went through three different interviews and got hired that same morning.

"The money and benefits were good and I figured I'd just work part time through the summer. I started nights and went to school part time during the day, paying my own way. Eventually I finished my degree and got a B.A. in law enforcement from the University of Houston.

"Originally, I had planned to work with juveniles, but there was no money involved there. Even though money wasn't my main interest, I figured that down the line I'd have to get a master's degree in order to get a decent salary. I talked to a lot of people working in law enforcement, too, and they pretty much talked me out of going for an interview with the police department. I don't regret it. I think I would have gotten too involved. I decided I was happy at the post office. I enjoy my work; I'm pretty content with it."

Expert Advice

"To be honest with you I'd say come in, do your work and leave, and hope you enjoy what you're doing. Don't get involved. Too much goes on. There's a lot of favoritism. Pressure. There are other jobs that maybe pay a few dollars less but have the same benefits. You'd probably be a lot happier."

•   •   •

INTERVIEW
Nick Delia
Letter Carrier

Nick Delia and his wife are both letter carriers. Nick has been working for the Postal Service for more than twelve years.

What the Job Is Really Like

"You have to rely on your memory a lot in this job. You get to know who is living at a certain address, who's a forward. Forwarding the mail is the responsibility of the letter carrier.

"The majority of my route is a business route, which means you're constantly in and out of the truck. For example, the local newspaper is on my route. I pull up to the building, take out their buckets of mail, then take them into the mailroom, and then get back into the truck and go to the next stop.

"I start at 6:00 in the morning. When I get in, most of the mail is already there. There are other clerks that get in at 3:00 or 4:00 in the morning. We have to first count our mail. It's counted by the foot. A certain number of letters makes up a foot. They come to you in trays and there are two feet of mail, the letter size, stacked on a tray. Then you've got your magazines and newspapers. You need to know how many feet you have. That's how the amount of time you need to deliver the mail is calculated. In my particular case, fifteen feet of mail would equal an eight-hour day. Anything over that, I'd need some overtime hours or some help.

"Then you have to go through all your mail, piece by piece, to check for forwards or holds. After that, you have to put the mail into this large case we have, with all sorts of separations. You check the name and the address, and then put it into the correct slot. When all your mail is up, you receive your accountable mail, your certified and registered letters. These you have to write up because they have to be signed for by the customer. Then you have your mark-up mail. That's the 'moved, left no forwarding address' or 'attempted, addressee unknown,' that sort of thing. Then you pull all the mail out of the case and it comes out in the order you'll deliver it. After that, you bundle it up in rubber bands and then you pull out your parcels. Everything then goes out to your truck.

"This all takes about four hours. That's before you get out to the street. I'm usually out on the street by 10:00 A.M. It looks like the easiest job in the world, but most people have no idea what goes on behind the scenes. The delivery part is the easiest part of the day.

"But of course you have a lot to deal with on the street. That old saying, 'neither snow, nor sleet,' and all that is really true. It doesn't matter what the weather is; the mail has to go.

"But on the street is really the best part. In my case, I get to talk to a lot of people; you see the same people every day and you get to know them. The mailman really knows a lot about you. He knows about your family, what you do for a living, where your mail comes from. We know it all. And everybody is always happy to see us. We're like a friend coming to visit.

"We get the opportunity to put in a lot of overtime if we want, maybe even an extra $10,000 a year, and the base top pay for a letter carrier here is pretty good, about $35,400. But we earn our money. Not in every job do you have a dog chasing you down the street or you're working through a lightning storm. And we have traffic to deal with, too, and kids running out in the street. We've got our hazards.

"Dealing with management feels like another hazard. Post office management is not known for being too bright, to be honest with you. And a lot of people just don't care about their job. They feel they can't make a difference. It's a government job; they collect their salary and benefits and that's it.

"And there are conflicts and sometimes violence in the post office. It's been in the papers. No one's pulled a gun where I work, but we have our problems.

"But, basically, I think it's a good job. I get a feeling of accomplishment on my job. At the beginning of the day, there's mail everywhere, but by the end of the day, there's nothing left; it's done. And I enjoy working outside, which is half of the job. I couldn't be a clerk, working indoors all day. The people are friendlier toward the letter carrier than they are to a window clerk."

How Nick Delia Got Started

"I had some family members who were already in the post office. My last job, working for U-Haul, was going nowhere. They were giving the test to work at the post office so I said, let's try it. It was basically a memory test, which has a lot to do with the job. I was called and started about twelve years ago."

Expert Advice

"You've got to be physically fit. You've got to enjoy being around other people. It really helps if you're outgoing.

"In addition, this is basically an unskilled job. Of course, you need a good memory and have to be intelligent, but if a person is not inclined to go to college, then this would be a good job."

•   •   •

FOR MORE INFORMATION

Local post offices and state employment service offices can supply details about entrance examinations and specific employment opportunities for postal clerks and mail carriers.

CHAPTER 7 The Foreign Service

EDUCATION
B.A./B.S. and
other education required

$$$ SALARY
$26,700–$116,000

OVERVIEW

A career serving one's country overseas can offer excitement, challenge, and even glamour. Members of the Foreign Service, which is under the jurisdiction of the United States Department of State, can travel the world and, at the same time, gain the satisfaction of helping other people and representing the interests of their country.

Being a part of the Foreign Service is more than just a job. It is a complete way of life that requires dedication and commitment. For those smart enough and tough enough to get the job done, the Foreign Service might be just the right place.

POSITIONS

The Foreign Service divides the different specialty areas into the following "cones."

Administration

Administrative personnel at overseas posts are responsible for hiring foreign national workers, providing office and residential space, assuring reliable communications with Washington, D.C., supervising computer systems, and—of great importance in hostile or unfriendly areas—providing security for posts' personnel and property.

Consular Services

Consular workers must often combine the skills of lawyers, judges, investigators, and social workers. Their duties range from issuing passports and visas to finding lost children or helping travelers in trouble.

Economic Officers

Economic officers maintain contact with key business and financial leaders in the host country and report to Washington on the local economic conditions and their impact on U.S. trade and investment policies. They are concerned with issues such as commercial aviation safety, fishing rights, and international banking.

Political Affairs

Those working in political affairs analyze and report on the political views of the host country. They make contact with labor unions, humanitarian organizations, educators, and cultural leaders.

Information and Cultural Affairs

As part of the Foreign Service, the United States Information Agency (USIA) promotes U.S. cultural, informational, and public diplomacy programs. An information officer might develop a library for the public, meet with the press, and oversee English language training programs for the host country.

Commercial and Business Services

In this division, a Foreign Service officer identifies overseas business connections for U.S. exporters and investors, conducts market research for the success of U.S. products, and organizes trade shows and other promotional events.

Foreign Service officers can be based in Washington, D.C., or can be sent anywhere in the world. They work at embassies, consulates, and other diplomatic missions in major cities or small towns. They help the thousands of Americans traveling and living overseas, issue visas to citizens of other countries wishing to visit the United States, and help our government execute our foreign policies.

The Foreign Service officer accepts direction from the president of the United States and his or her top appointees. The main goal is to make U.S. policies succeed. He or she is expected to place loyalty over personal opinions and preferences.

Foreign Service workers can experience a glamourous lifestyle, dining with their ambassadors in European palaces, meeting royalty or other heads of state. They can be present at important decision-making sessions and influence world politics and history.

But postings can offer hardship as well, in environments as hostile as Antarctica or a Middle Eastern desert. Some assignments, or postings, are in isolated locations without all the familiar comforts of home. The weather can be harsh, and there can be health hazards. Danger from unrest or war is often present.

In spite of the difficulties, many in the Foreign Service are happy with the unique rewards and opportunities.

TRAINING

Although many Foreign Service officers are skilled in political science and history, candidates these days also can have knowledge in specialized fields such as the environment, computer science, the fight against AIDS, antidrug efforts, and trade.

There are several steps to complete in order to apply for a position in the Foreign Service.

Written Examination

This is a day-long multiple choice test usually given once a year. It measures verbal and numerical reasoning, political and cultural awareness, English-language expression, and knowledge of topics important to the function of the Foreign Service. It's a difficult exam, and many people have to take it more than once before they pass.

Oral Evaluation

Those who pass the written exam will be invited to participate in an all-day oral assessment. It tests the skills, abilities, knowledge, and personal characteristics necessary to succeed in the Foreign Service. Writing skills are also measured, as are administrative, problem-solving, leadership, and interpersonal skills.

Medical Clearance

Because many postings have inadequate health care or pose health hazards, candidates for the Foreign Service must meet a high medical standard. Allowances are made, however, for certain handicaps.

Background Investigation

The State Department, along with other federal, state, and local agencies, conducts a thorough background check on Foreign Service candidates. The check includes examination of employment records, credit history, repayment of school loans, drug abuse, and criminal records.

ELIGIBILITY

Before a person can take the Foreign Service written examination, he or she must be

- at least twenty years old on the date of the exam

- no more than fifty-nine years old

- a citizen of the United States

- available for worldwide assignment

JOB OUTLOOK

The Foreign Service exam is not always offered on a yearly basis––the exam is given when there are positions to fill. Because competition is keen for all positions with the Foreign Service, the number of candidates tends to always exceed the number of openings. Most openings arise from the need to replace Foreign Service workers who retire or leave the profession for other reasons.

SALARIES

The starting salary is generally low, but it may be increased at overseas posts with free housing, furniture and utilities, travel expenses, educational allowances for children, and cost-of-living allowances in high-cost cities. Extra pay is also given for dangerous and "hardship" posts.

RELATED FIELDS

There are many different areas in which to work in the Foreign Service, and each area requires its own set of skills and background. Foreign Service administrators perform functions similar to those of general managers and others in supervisory positions. Economic officers and business and commercial officers utilize skills found in the business world in market research and in public relations. Consuls often possess the same skills important to lawyers, judges, investigators, and social workers. Information officers have duties similar to those of a press secretary.

INTERVIEW
Jim Van Laningham
General Services Officer

Jim Van Laningham has made the Foreign Service his career for more than fifteen years. He's been posted in Russia in the former Soviet Union, Poland, Morocco, Iraq, and Washington, D.C. He is a general service officer, a position that falls under the Administration cone.

What the Job Is Really Like

"An administrative officer is the person responsible for keeping the embassy operating on a day-to-day basis. First thing in the morning I might find a series of cables from Washington waiting for me, which would require me to report on certain information. Depending on the time of the year, I may be involved in renewing leases on houses we rent for our American staff or I may be involved in preparing the budget for the embassy, which could be anywhere from a million dollars up. The budget covers salaries of embassy staff, electricity and other utilities, procurement of paper and pencils, and computers, copy machines, and other office equipment.

"For lunch I may meet with several of my counterparts from other embassies, administrative officers from Australia or Canada or Great Britain, to discuss issues.

"Later on in the day, I may be involved in some personnel issues where I evaluate employee performance and recommend promotion. Or I may have a discipline problem with an employee and have to talk to him or her about it. I'm even responsible for having to fire someone if necessary.

"Entertaining is a big part of a Foreign Service officer's life—either having local people or people from other embassies to dinner or going to dinner at someone else's house. Oftentimes, you learn a lot about what's going on in the country from talking to other diplomats or the people who live there.

"On weekends you can travel around the country, go to other cities and see what there is to see, not only just to play tourist, but to meet other people and talk to them.

"What I like most about being an administrative officer in the Foreign Service is the opportunity to see a problem, determine what the solution is, and then see it through to the end. Obviously, travel is also a very attractive part of the job. You can live overseas in a country for a number of years and really get to know what it's like in depth.

"And for me there's a lot of excitement about being able to represent the United States overseas, meeting important people in the country where you are living and perhaps even affecting how relations develop between the United States and that country.

"I was posted in Iraq at the time Saddam Hussein invaded Kuwait. I had been scheduled to fly home to attend my high school reunion, but of course there were no planes leaving the country and I couldn't get out.

"We were able to evacuate most of the staff of the American Embassy in Baghdad, and then we had about 100 people from the embassy in Kuwait who were trying to get back to the United States. Although originally we were given permission for them to leave, it turned out they were not able to. A lot of my time for about three days was spent trying to get exit visas. The permission finally came through at about 3:00 in the morning, Iraqi time.

"I suddenly remembered that that was the exact time my high school reunion had been scheduled. I knew the telephone number where the reunion was being held, so I called and ended up talking to about forty of my former classmates over the phone. Between that and having just succeeded in getting visas for 100 people to get out of the country, it made a wonderful experience, one that I won't quickly forget.

"Another benefit working with the Foreign Service is that you can retire at age fifty with twenty years of service.

"There are always some downsides, however. When you have a very large organization like the State Department and you have a lot of different officers with various interests, and you're working on a problem where it's necessary to get the approval of all those officers on any action you want to take, it can be time-consuming and frustrating.

"And as the U.S. government faces a shrinking budget and the State Department faces a shrinking budget, there's less money to get things accomplished with.

"But as frustrating as it can be at times, it's a fabulous career. There's no such thing as a regular routine and every day you can have a new challenge in front of you. For me it's a fun way of life."

How Jim Van Laningham Got Started

"Originally, I became interested about the time I was in junior high school. I had just read the book *The Ugly American*, and it talked about the image of Americans overseas and how Foreign Service officers helped correct what often was a bad image. It got me thinking about it. Eventually, I took the Foreign Service exam and I got in.

"I earned a bachelor's degree in economics and then went on for a master's in international business. I took the exam right after I graduated and all the information was still fresh. My education was very helpful.

"It was a year and a half from the time I took the exam until I got accepted. I was very excited. They called me up one day and asked if I could be there in less than a month. They wanted an answer right away. My wife and I discussed it and decided to take the plunge. We went to Washington and they gave me about two months of training in a basic orientation course for new officers and six months of language training.

"After that I was assigned to the embassy in Moscow as an economics officer. But today it's almost mandatory that the first tour for most foreign service officers is as a consular officer, issuing visas to people who want to come to the United States."

Expert Advice

"You have to be able to write well, to organize thoughts logically and coherently. You have to be outgoing because you deal with a lot of different people and you have to have people skills. I think you have to be interested in the world and what's going on around you, because a lot of what you do is reporting back to Washington on what's happening in the country you're in.

"And if you're in the administration cone, hopefully you are a good manager of people. You have to have leadership ability. It also helps to be familiar with finances and budgets.

"But I don't think there's any one particular field of study that leads to the Foreign Service. The people I've met have taken every imaginable major in school. It's more just studying well and doing well and getting a well-rounded education."

•   •   •

INTERVIEW
Robert Manzanares
Administrative Officer

Bob Manzanares entered the Foreign Service in 1978. He has held a variety of positions including consular officer, general services officer, chief of post management for the Middle Eastern Bureau, and director for the Office of Administration for the National Security Council.

He has been posted in the Ivory Coast, West Africa, Mexico, Iceland, Israel, and Washington, D.C.

What the Job Is Really Like

"I was a consular officer in Mexico City, which was known as a 'visa mill.' Everyone wanted to come to the United States and by 8:00 in the morning we would have between 2,000 and 3,000 people waiting in this huge line to enter the compound and apply for a visa. I was one of fourteen officers working in a little *casita*, a makeshift hut, and we would listen to each applicant for a minute to a minute and a half and make a decision whether or not to issue a visa. This would go on nonstop from 8:00 to 2:00 and we would process more than 4,000 applications a day.

"In the afternoon we would issue visas with passports that came in through a tourist agency. It was the same work but not as interesting because we didn't get to talk to the people.

"I also made prison visits. Occasionally, we have Americans who wind up in prison, for whatever reasons, and so my job was to go in and make sure they were not being abused and that they had access to an attorney.

"Also, if an American should die overseas, the consular officer has to contact the family and make arrangements to ship the body home.

"When I was with the Middle Eastern Bureau in Washington, I was one of the main organizers, from the logistical side, of the Middle East Peace Talks that took place in Madrid. Working with a team, I helped organize the conference site and coordinated all the different arrangements that go into putting together a conference like that, from security to transportation to hotels to interpreters—the whole gamut.

"I like the flexibility of being able to change jobs and locations every so often. Before I joined the Foreign Service, I worked for six years in city administration. That was fun, but I couldn't see myself doing that for twenty years.

"The most difficult aspect of working in the Foreign Service is leaving behind all the people you've met. For the short period of time you're posted in a country, you get to know people there, they become your friends, your new family during holidays, and then you move on to the next post and it's easy to lose touch."

How Bob Manzanares Got Started

"While I was in graduate school studying public administration, I met a State Department employee. He had just served in Peru and spoke perfect Spanish. I was amazed at his language capabilities because, even with my Hispanic background, he was showing me up badly. I asked him how he had become so proficient, and he told me about the Foreign Service.

"I was attracted to all the stories he told, the languages, the cultures, the travel, and on a lark I decided to take the test, not thinking I would pass. And in fact I didn't pass the first time. I tried again and then I was successful."

Expert Advice

"Get a liberal arts background if you can and have some experience before you try to get in. There's a lot of what I call *trench time*—it's a structured bureaucracy and you have to go through the steps to get to the top. Those people who come in with a little more life experience, not necessarily just work experience, fare better.

"It's a competitive service all the way around. There's competition for promotions; there's competition for different postings. It keeps you on your toes.

"You have to like people and be willing to accept and live among other cultures. There are inconveniences, but you should be flexible and not expect to transplant America with you when you go overseas. I remember when I was a junior officer on my way for my first tour to the Ivory Coast. I think there had just been a coup in Ghana, and when a Ghanian airplane landed in Sierra Leone, the officials would not gas it up. They discharged all the passengers and left all the baggage on the runway and then took off. I had been planning to get on that plane—it was the only one scheduled to the Ivory Coast—but I got stuck in the chaos at the airport for fourteen hours waiting for the next flight out. Not everything operates the way you'd expect. When you want to fly in West Africa, you just have to go with the flow.

"Sometimes I'm reminded of how much I love my country when I've been overseas for a year or eighteen months and I haven't been home in all that time. Maybe we've been expecting a congressional delegation or a presidential visit and you see that American plane coming in with the United States of America painted on its side and the big American flag on the back. I watch it land and it always brings chills up my spine.

"And to see the host country's people in awe of what we have, it makes me wish sometimes that Americans could learn to appreciate their own country more."

●   ●   ●

FOR MORE INFORMATION

For more information on careers in the Foreign Service, write to

Department of State
Recruitment Division
P.O. Box 9317
Rosslyn Station
Arlington, VA 22209
1-800-JOB-OVERSEAS

CHAPTER 8 Engineers with the Government

EDUCATION
B.A./B.S. degree required

$$$ SALARY
$29,000-$55,000

OVERVIEW

Federal, state, and local governments employ about 181,000 engineers. Over half of these work for the federal government, mainly in the departments of Defense, Transportation, Agriculture, Interior, and Energy and in the National Aeronautics and Space Administration.

Most engineers in state and local government agencies work in highway and public works departments. Some engineers are self-employed consultants.

Engineers are employed in every state, in small and large cities, and in rural areas. Some branches of engineering are concentrated in particular industries and geographic areas.

Engineers apply the theories and principles of science and mathematics to the economical solution of practical technical problems. Often their work is the link between a scientific discovery and its application. Engineers design machinery, products, systems, and processes for efficient and economical performance. They design industrial machinery and equipment for manufacturing goods and defense and weapons systems for the Armed Forces. Many engineers design, plan, and supervise the construction of buildings, highways, and rapid transit systems. They also design and develop consumer products and systems for control and automation of manufacturing, business, and management processes.

Engineers consider many factors in developing new products. For example, in developing an industrial robot, they determine precisely what function it needs to perform; design and test components; fit them together in an integrated plan; and evaluate the design's overall effectiveness, cost, reliability, and safety. This process applies to products as different as computers, gas turbines, generators, helicopters, and toys.

In addition to working in design and development, engineers may work in testing, production, or maintenance. They supervise production in factories, determine the causes of breakdowns, and test manufactured products to maintain quality. They also estimate the time and cost to complete projects.

Engineers often use computers to simulate and test how machines, structures, or systems operate. Many engineers also use computer-assisted design systems to produce and analyze designs. They also spend a great deal of time writing reports and consulting with other engineers.

Complex projects require many engineers, each working with a small part of the job. Supervisory engineers are responsible for major components or entire projects.

SPECIALIZATIONS

Most engineers specialize; more than twenty-five major specialties are recognized by professional societies. Within the major branches are numerous subdivisions. For example, structural engineering, transportation engineering, and environmental engineering—a small but growing discipline involved with identifying, solving, and alleviating environmental problems—are subdivisions of civil engineering.

Engineers also may specialize in one industry, such as motor vehicles, or in one field of technology, such as propulsion or guidance systems. Here is a partial list of engineering specializations:

Aerospace

Architectural

Biomedical

Chemical

Civil

Computer engineering

Electrical and electronics

Industrial

Marine

Materials, metallurgical, and ceramic

Mechanical

Mining

Nuclear

Petroleum

Engineers in each branch have knowledge and training that can be applied to many fields. Electrical and electronics engineers, for example, work in the medical, computer, missile guidance, and power distribution fields. Because there are many separate problems to solve in a large engineering project, engineers in one field often work closely with specialists in scientific, other engineering, and business occupations.

WORKING CONDITIONS

Many engineers work in laboratories, industrial plants, or construction sites, where they inspect, supervise, or solve on-site problems. Others work in offices almost all of the time.

Engineers in branches such as civil engineering may work outdoors part of the time. A few engineers travel extensively to plants or construction sites.

Many engineers work standard forty-hour weeks. At times, deadlines or design standards may bring extra pressure to a job. When this happens, engineers may work long hours and experience considerable stress.

TRAINING

A bachelor's degree in engineering from an accredited engineering program is usually required for beginning engineering jobs. College graduates with a degree in a physical science or in mathematics may qualify for some engineering jobs, especially in engineering specialties in high demand. Most engineering degrees are granted in branches such as electrical, mechanical, or civil engineering. However, engineers trained in one branch may work in another. This flexibility allows employers to meet staffing needs in new technologies and specialties in short supply. It also allows engineers to shift to fields with better employment prospects or ones that match their interests more closely.

In addition to granting the standard engineering degree, many colleges grant degrees in engineering technology, which are offered as either two- or four-year programs. These programs prepare students for practical design and production work rather than for jobs that require more theoretical, scientific, and mathematical knowledge. Graduates of four-year technology programs may get jobs similar to those obtained by graduates with bachelor's degrees in engineering. In fact, some employers regard them as having skills between those of technicians and engineers.

Graduate training is essential for engineering faculty positions but is not required for the majority of entry level engineering jobs. Many engineers obtain master's degrees to learn new technology, to broaden their education, and to enhance promotion opportunities.

Nearly 340 colleges and universities offer a bachelor's degree in engineering, and nearly 300 colleges offer a bachelor's degree in engineering technology, although not all are accredited programs. Although most institutions offer programs in the larger branches of engineering, only a few offer some of the smaller specialties.

Also, programs of the same title may vary in content. For example, some emphasize industrial practices, preparing students for jobs in industry, while others are more theoretical and are better for students preparing to take graduate work. Therefore, students should investigate curriculums and check accreditations carefully before selecting a college. Admissions requirements for undergraduate engineering schools include courses in advanced high school mathematics and the physical sciences.

Bachelor's degree programs in engineering are typically designed to last four years, but many students find that it takes between four and five years to complete their studies. In a typical four-year college curriculum, the first two years are spent studying basic sciences (mathematics, physics, and chemistry), introductory engineering, and the humanities, social sciences, and English. In the last two years, most courses are in engineering, usually with a concentration in one branch. For example, the last two years of an aerospace program might include courses such as fluid mechanics, heat transfer, applied aerodynamics, analytical mechanics, flight vehicle design, trajectory dynamics, and aerospace propulsion systems. Some programs offer a general engineering curriculum; students then specialize in graduate school or on the job.

A few engineering schools and two-year colleges have agreements whereby the two-year colleges provide the initial engineering education and the engineering schools automatically admit students for their last two years. In addition, a few engineering schools have arrangements whereby students spend three years in liberal arts college studying pre-engineering subjects and two years in engineering school and receive bachelor's degrees from each. Some colleges and universities offer five-year master's degree programs.

Some five- or even six-year cooperative plans combine classroom study and practical work, permitting students to gain valuable experience and finance part of their education.

All fifty states and the District of Columbia require registration for engineers whose work may affect life, health, or property or who offer their services to the public. In 1992, nearly 380,000 engineers were registered. Registration generally requires a degree from an engineering program accredited by the Accreditation Board for Engineering and Technology, four years of relevant work experience, and successful completion of a state examination. Some states will not register people with degrees in engineering technology.

Engineers should be able to work as part of a team and should have creativity, analytical minds, and a capacity for detail. In addition, engineers should be able to express themselves well both orally and in writing.

Beginning engineering graduates usually do routine work under the supervision of experienced engineers and, in large companies, may also receive formal classroom or seminar-type training. As they gain knowledge and experience, they are assigned more difficult tasks with greater independence to develop designs, solve problems, and make decisions.

Engineers may become technical specialists or may supervise staffs or teams of engineers and technicians. Some eventually become engineering managers or enter managerial, management support, or sales jobs.

Some engineers obtain graduate degrees in engineering or business administration to improve advancement opportunities; others obtain law degrees and become patent attorneys. Many high-level executives in government and industry began their careers as engineers.

JOB OUTLOOK

In 1994, engineers held 1,327,000 jobs. Just under one-half of all engineering jobs were located in manufacturing industries, mostly in electrical and electronic equipment, aircraft and parts, industrial machinery, scientific instruments, chemicals, motor vehicles, guided missiles and space vehicles, fabricated metal products, and primary metals industries.

In 1994, 684,000 jobs were in nonmanufacturing industries, primarily in engineering and architectural services, research and testing services, and business services, in which firms designed construction projects or did other engineering work on a contract basis for organizations in other parts of the economy. Engineers also worked in the communications, utilities, and construction industries.

Employment opportunities in engineering have been good for a number of years. Through the year 2005 employment is expected to increase about as fast as the average for all occupations, while the number of degrees granted in engineering is expected to remain near present levels.

Many of the jobs in engineering are related to national defense. Defense expenditures have declined, so employment growth and the job outlook for engineers may not be as strong as in times when defense expenditures were increasing. However, graduating engineers will continue to be in demand for jobs in engineering and other areas, possibly even at the same time that other engineers, especially defense industry engineers, are being laid off.

Employers will rely on engineers to further increase productivity as they increase investment in plants and equipment to expand output of goods and services. In addition, competitive pressures and advancing technology will force companies to improve and update product designs more frequently. Finally, more engineers will be needed to improve deteriorating roads, bridges, water and pollution control systems, and other public facilities.

Freshman engineering enrollments began declining in 1983, and the number of bachelor's degrees in engineering began declining in 1987. Although it is difficult to project engineering enrollments, this decline may continue through the late 1990s because the total college-age population is projected to decline.

Furthermore, the proportion of students interested in engineering careers has declined as prospects for college graduates in other fields have improved and interest in other programs has increased.

Only a relatively small number of engineers leaves the profession each year. Despite this, three-fourths of all job openings will arise from replacement needs. A greater number of replacement openings is created by engineers who transfer to management, sales, or other professional specialty occupations than by those who leave the labor force.

Most industries are less likely to lay off engineers than other workers. Many engineers work on long-term research and development projects or on other activities that may continue even during recessions. In industries such as electronics and aerospace, however, large government cutbacks in defense or research and development have resulted in layoffs for engineers.

New computer-assisted design systems enable engineers to produce or modify designs much more rapidly than previously. This increased productivity might have resulted in fewer engineering jobs had engineers not used these systems to improve the design process. They now produce and analyze many more design variations before selecting a final one. Therefore, this technology is not expected to limit employment opportunities.

It is important for engineers to continue their education throughout their careers because much of their value to their employers depends on their knowledge of the latest technology. In 1990, about 110,000 persons, or 7.5 percent of all engineers, were enrolled in graduate engineering programs. The pace of technological change varies by engineering specialty and industry. Engineers in high-technology areas, such as advanced electronics or aerospace, may find that their knowledge becomes obsolete rapidly. Even the jobs of those who continue their education are vulnerable to obsolescence if the particular technology or product they have specialized in becomes obsolete. Engineers whom employers consider not to have kept up may find themselves passed over for promotions and are particularly vulnerable to layoffs.

On the other hand, it is often these high-technology areas that offer the greatest challenges, the most interesting work, and the highest salaries. Therefore, the choice of engineering specialty and employer involves an assessment not only of the potential rewards but also of the risk of technological obsolescence.

SALARIES

The average annual salary for engineers in the federal government in nonsupervisory, supervisory, and managerial positions was $58,080 in 1995.

Starting salaries for engineers with bachelor's degrees are significantly higher than starting salaries of bachelor's degree graduates in other fields. According to the National Association of Colleges and Employers, engineering graduates with bachelor's degrees averaged about $34,100 a year in private industry in 1994; those with master's degrees and no experience, $40,200 a year; and those with Ph.D. degrees, $55,300.

A survey of workplaces in 160 metropolitan areas reported that beginning engineers had median annual earnings of about $33,900 in 1993, with the middle half earning between about $30,900 and $36,900 a year. Experienced midlevel engineers with no supervisory responsibilities had median annual earnings of about $54,400, with the middle half earning between about $49,800 and $59,600 a year. Median annual earnings for engineers at senior managerial levels were about $90,000.

For those with bachelor's degrees, starting salaries vary by branch, as shown in the following chart:

Chemical	$39,204
Petroleum	38,286
Mechanical	35,051
Electrical	34,840
Nuclear	33,603
Materials	33,429
Industrial	33,267
Mining	32,638
Aerospace	30,860
Civil	29,809

RELATED FIELDS

Engineers apply the principles of physical science and mathematics in their work. Other workers who use scientific and mathematical principles are physical scientists, life scientists, computer scientists, mathematicians, engineering and science technicians, and architects.

INTERVIEW
Timothy Sikora
Aerospace Engineer

Timothy Sikora is a civilian aerospace engineer working for the U.S. Air Force at the Wright Laboratory, Flight Dynamics Directorate, Structures Division, Wright-Patterson AFB in Ohio. He earned his B.S. in mechanical engineering (B.S.M.E.) from the University of Akron in Ohio in 1980.

What the Job Is Really Like

"I'm a civilian working for the Air Force. In the laboratory environment where I am, it is probably 95 percent civilian and

5 percent military, not including on-site contractors who are all civilian. There are definite advantages to being a civilian instead of military: we don't get transferred every four years; we can keep doing the same sort of job without having to 'diversify' like the military; in time of war we're not in a desert foxhole being shelled; there are no uniforms, saluting, base housing, etc.

"The military come through our organization to 'fill blocks' in their career briefs, but we consider them part-time help. But they are very appreciated because their payroll doesn't come out of lab funds, so we get good technical support at basically no cost.

"We work according to projects that have been set up by our organization in support of other Air Force organizations with funding. Any Air Force organization that has an aircraft or a new technology that requires structural testing to verify a design, determine a weakness, or evaluate a repair can present us with the program. As a project engineer, I have to analyze the test program to determine the best way to conduct the test to meet the customer's needs. I then work up a cost estimate for us to charge the customer for the test. (For many years we were only allowed to work for other government agencies, mostly Department of Defense or NASA. Sometimes a contractor had need of our facilities for a contract they were working on. They would have to turn back some of their contract dollars to the government agency funding them. Then the government agency would use those funds to pay us to do the test—complicated paper shuffle, really. Recently we've been authorized to work directly for private industry, but a few test cases ended up in such legal tangles that they've put the program on hold.)

"If the estimate is within their budget, and they approve of our test proposal, they agree to fund the program. I then have to perform a detailed setup design for the test. In some cases, this requires creativity and technology development. We are a research and development organization, so we always try to improve the state of testing technology. I have the responsibility to ensure that the test is set up correctly, on time, and within budget. I then have to conduct the test. Some tests can be completed in one day, after six months of setting up. Some tests are durability tests that run two shifts, five days a week, for several years.

"Through all of this, I work with a team of other engineers, technicians, and mechanics. They have specialties and, as project engineer, I oversee all of it. At the conclusion of the test, I have to report on the test results and any new technology that was developed as part of the test program.

"The work varies from frantic and hectic to relaxed and patient. Sometimes everything is on hold while we wait for the test article delivery, which is late, or we're working at breakneck pace because there's an emergency in the fleet that needs solving right away.

"The aspect that I enjoy the most is developing new technology or conducting a test that's never been done before—the challenge of applying something new and making it work. The least favorite part is the paperwork. The work is only boring when the bureaucratic paperwork has to be done. The financial tracking, the environmental protection, and the acquisition training all have tedious procedures that have to be followed."

How Timothy Sikora Got Started

"I've always wanted to be a scientist and to invent something new, to be at the cutting edge of new technology, to live in the state of the art. As I got older, I learned that pure scientists don't always get to bring new concepts to reality. Many scientists are purely theoretical; they invent on paper. I learned that engineers make new concepts into usable reality.

"Also many engineers are creating new concepts and ideas, working in conjunction with many of the pure scientists. I selected mechanical engineering to major in because it makes heavy use of physics, which was my favorite physical science. I've had special interest in vehicles, ways of getting from here to there. The space program held special fascination and awe for me.

"Aerospace engineering is a specialization under mechanical engineering. (An aeroengineer would probably disagree ferociously, but what do they know?) Akron University did not have an aerospace engineering program, but even if they did, I would still have gone into mechanical engineering because the M.E. degree is more marketable. A lot of aerospace engineers had lost their jobs by the time I graduated due to the cancellation of the

Supersonic Transport program and cutbacks in the space program, so I was leery of specializing. For the type of aerospace engineering I'm doing, I would not have used any aeronautical courses and have used many mechanical courses that the aero-engineers didn't have.

"I started cooperative education in summer of 1977 with the U.S. Navy. I knew that the co-op program offered the best of both the educational world and the workplace. I tried hiring into NASA, but they were under a hiring freeze at that time. I took the job with the Navy, outside Washington, D.C., because my brother worked there and I knew they did interesting work. After three years, on and off in the co-op program, I decided that, although I really liked the work I was doing, the hassles and cost of living in the D.C. area weren't worth it.

"During my senior year in college I interviewed with the Air Force, hoping to get a job similar to what I did with the Navy. I interviewed around the base with different organizations. The Structures Test Lab was very similar to what I did with the Navy, but I wanted to make sure I didn't miss another opportunity. I asked to come back to interview at some more places, and to reinterview with the Structures Test Lab. I decided that I liked it and they made me a job offer. At that time they were hungry for qualified engineers; it was really a graduates' market.

"By taking a job with the Air Force, near Dayton, Ohio, at the same salary, I was effectively getting a raise by living in a less expensive locale."

Expert Advice

"Although education and the degree are essential for landing a job, to be proficient in the job requires experience. Actual working in the engineering environment is invaluable to the engineer. Quite literally, 90 percent of my education came from the job. Don't think that the university atmosphere is any substitute for working in the real world.

"The other key characteristic to success is imagination. Being able to relate some obscure fact you read three years ago to a present-day problem could provide the solution. Sometimes a leap of imagination is needed to jump a hurdle."

INTERVIEW
Brian Adams
Electronic Systems Engineer

●　●　●

Brian Adams works at Lockheed Martin Vought Systems Corporation in Grand Prairie, Texas, specializing in electronic technologies. This division of Lockheed is a Department of Defense contractor specializing in missile systems.

Brian Adams earned a B.S. in forestry at Stephen F. Austin State University, in Nacogdoches, Texas, in 1980 and then later decided to pursue engineering as a career instead. He earned his B.S. in electrical engineering from the University of Texas in Arlington in 1994. He began working full time as an electrical engineer in 1995.

What the Job Is Really Like

"LMVS uses what they call a *9/80 work schedule*. Monday through Thursday you work nine-hour days for a total of thirty-six hours. On alternating Fridays, you work eight hours. This gives alternating Fridays off.

"In my group, we primarily do microwave radio frequency design for a missile communication system. The atmosphere can alternate from hectic and fast-paced to slow and a little boring, depending on the stage of development we are in. It is interesting if not a little frustrating sometimes. Being the new kid, I perceive a lot of what we do as akin to black magic, and it is very difficult to comprehend. For that matter, no one else in the company understands what we do either, which can make for some pretty interesting clashes when our needs conflict with the needs of others.

"I've made a lot of good friends at work and I think that is what I like most. We're all EEs and, consequently, we have a lot of the same interests—we like to take things apart and see if we can successfully put them back together again. My computer, for instance, is one I put together with the help of my wife.

"What I don't like is that I have to drive almost into Dallas to get to work—that's too far. In fact, most of the high-tech companies are in North Dallas, so I guess I was lucky to get one so close to home."

How Brian Adams Got Started

"My wife pursued this field before I did, and I had come to a crossroads in my professional life where I was trying to figure out my next move. At the time, I had just finished working for Tandy Corporation to work at a small company in Arlington called *Altai*, which specialized in computer operating systems scheduling software. That didn't work out for me at all and only lasted three months. My wife suggested that EE was right up my alley and that I would be a natural for it. I took her advice and graduated with a 3.9 GPA.

"My current job is my first job after graduating from the University of Texas at Arlington. I started out as an EE co-op student. Co-ops go to work for a company in their sophomore or junior year and from then on alternate between a semester of school and a semester of work. I co-oped for four terms before graduating. Upon graduation, Lockheed (at the time they were called *Loral Vought*) hired me full time."

Expert Advice

"Attend school at a well-known institution (University of Texas at Austin or A&M in Texas, for instance). That is where the best recruiting is taking place. If you settle on a smaller, lesser-known place like the University of Texas at Arlington, your choices will be severely limited. There are a lot of neat things happening out there and as far as interesting work goes, engineering has it."

●   ●   ●

FOR MORE INFORMATION

High school students interested in obtaining general information on a variety of engineering disciplines should contact the Junior Engineering Technical Society by sending a self-addressed, stamped business size envelope with six first-class stamps to

JETS—Guidance
1420 King Street, Suite 405
Alexandria, VA 22314

Write the following professional associations for each engineering specialization.

American Chemical Society
Career Services
1155 16th Street NW
Washington, DC 20036

American Institute of Aeronautics and Astronautics
AIAA Student Programs
The Aerospace Center
370 L'Enfant Promenade SW
Washington, DC 20024-2518

American Institute of Chemical Engineers
345 East 47th Street
New York, NY 10017

American Nuclear Society
555 North Kensington Avenue
LaGrange Park, IL 60525

Institute of Electrical and Electronics Engineers
1828 L Street NW, Suite 1202
Washington, DC 20036

Institute of Industrial Engineers
25 Technology Park/Atlanta
Norcross, GA 30092

American Society of Civil Engineers
345 E. 47th Street
New York, NY 10017

The American Society of Mechanical Engineers
345 E. 47th Street
New York, NY 10017

American Society of Heating, Refrigerating, and
Air-Conditioning Engineers
1791 Tullie Circle NE
Atlanta, GA 30329

Society of Petroleum Engineers
222 Palisades Creek Drive
Richardson, TX 75080

For information about engineering careers in the military, contact local recruiting stations for each branch.

CHAPTER 9 Social Services

![EDUCATION]
EDUCATION
B.A./B.S. degree required

$$$ SALARY
$30,000-$44,000

OVERVIEW

A wide range of professionals with titles such as *social worker* or *counselor* work for the government in various social service agencies. They help individuals cope with problems such as inadequate housing, unemployment, lack of job skills, financial mismanagement, serious illness, disability, substance abuse, unwanted pregnancy, and antisocial behavior. They also work with families that have serious conflicts, including those involving child or spousal abuse.

Through direct counseling, these professionals help clients identify their real concerns and help them consider solutions and find resources. Often, social service professionals provide concrete information about where to go for debt counseling, how to find child care or elder care, how to apply for public assistance or other benefits, or how to get an alcoholic or drug addict admitted to a rehabilitation program.

Social service professionals may also arrange for services in consultation with clients and then follow through to assure the services are actually helpful. They may review eligibility requirements, fill out forms and applications, visit clients on a regular basis, and step in during emergencies.

Rehabilitation counselors help people deal with the personal, social, and vocational impact of their disabilities. They evaluate the strengths and limitations of individuals, provide personal and vocational counseling, and arrange for medical care, vocational training, and job placement.

Rehabilitation counselors interview individuals with disabilities and their families, evaluate school and medical reports, and confer and plan with physicians, psychologists, occupational therapists, employers, and others. Conferring with clients, they develop and implement rehabilitation programs, which may include training to help clients become more independent and employable. They also work toward increasing clients' capacity to adjust and live independently.

Mental health counselors emphasize prevention and work with individuals and groups to promote optimum mental health. They help people deal with addictions and substance abuse; family, parenting, and marital problems; suicidal thoughts; stress management; problems with self-esteem; issues associated with aging; job and career concerns; educational decisions; and issues of mental and emotional health.

Mental health counselors work closely with other mental health specialists, including psychiatrists, psychologists, clinical social workers, psychiatric nurses, and school counselors.

Most social service workers specialize in particular clinical fields such as child welfare and family services, mental health, medical social work, or school social work. Clinical social workers offer psychotherapy or counseling and a range of services in public agencies, clinics, and private practice. Other social workers are employed in community organizations, administration, or research.

Social service professionals in child welfare or family services may counsel children and youths who have difficulty adjusting socially, advise parents on how to care for disabled children, or arrange for homemaker services during parents' illnesses. If children have serious problems in school, child welfare workers may consult with parents, teachers, and counselors to identify underlying causes and develop plans for treatment.

Some social service professionals assist single parents, arrange adoptions, and help find foster homes for neglected or abandoned children. Child welfare workers also work in residential institutions for children and adolescents.

Social workers in child or adult protective services investigate reports of abuse and neglect and intervene if necessary. They may institute legal action to remove children from homes and place them temporarily in emergency shelters or with foster families.

Social workers in criminal justice make recommendations to courts, conduct presentencing assessments, and provide services for prison inmates and their families. Probation and parole officers provide similar services to individuals on parole or sentenced by courts to probation.

Most social service professionals have a standard forty-hour week. However, they may work some evenings and weekends to meet with clients, attend community meetings, and handle emergencies.

The work, while satisfying, can be emotionally draining. Understaffing and large caseloads add to the pressure in some agencies.

TRAINING

A bachelor's degree is the minimum requirement for human service aide positions. Besides those with bachelor's degrees in social work (B.S.W.), undergraduate majors in psychology, sociology, and related fields satisfy hiring requirements in some agencies, especially small community agencies.

A master's degree in counseling or in social work (M.S.W.) is generally necessary for positions in health and mental health settings.

Generally, counselors working in government social services have master's degrees in substance-abuse counseling, rehabilitation counseling, agency or community counseling, mental health counseling, counseling psychology, career counseling, or related fields.

Graduate-level counselor education programs in colleges and universities usually are in departments of education or psychology. Courses are grouped into eight core areas:

human growth and development; social and cultural foundations; helping relationships; groups; lifestyle and career development; appraisal; research and evaluation; and professional orientation.

In an accredited program, forty-eight to sixty semester hours of graduate study, including a period of supervised clinical experience in counseling, are required for a master's degree.

The Council for Accreditation of Counseling and Related Educational Programs (CACREP) accredits graduate counseling programs in counselor education and in community, gerontological, mental health, school, student affairs, and marriage and family counseling.

In 1995, forty-one states and the District of Columbia had some form of counselor credentialing legislation requiring licensure, certification, or registry for practice outside schools. Requirements vary from state to state. In some states, credentialing is mandatory and in others, voluntary.

Many counselors elect to be nationally certified by the National Board for Certified Counselors (NBCC), which grants the general practice credential *national certified counselor*. In order to be certified, a counselor must hold a master's degree in counseling, have at least two years of professional counseling experience, and pass NBCC's National Counselor Examination. This national certification is voluntary and distinct from state certification.

However, in some states, those who pass the national exam are exempt from taking a state certification exam. NBCC also offers specialty certification in career, gerontological, school, and clinical mental health counseling.

Vocational and related rehabilitation agencies generally require a master's degree in rehabilitation counseling, counseling and guidance, or counseling psychology for rehabilitation counselor jobs. Some, however, may accept applicants with bachelor's degrees in rehabilitation services, counseling, psychology, or related fields.

A bachelor's degree in counseling qualifies a person to work as a counseling aide, rehabilitation aide, or social service worker. Experience in employment counseling, job development, psychology, education, or social work may be helpful.

The Council on Rehabilitation Education (CORE) accredits graduate programs in rehabilitation counseling. A minimum of two years of study, including a period of supervised clinical experience, are required for the master's degree. Some colleges and universities offer a bachelor's degree in rehabilitation services education.

In most state vocational rehabilitation agencies, applicants must pass a written examination and be evaluated by a board of examiners. Many employers require rehabilitation counselors to be certified. To become certified by the Commission on Rehabilitation Counselor Certification, counselors must graduate from an accredited educational program, complete an internship, and pass a written examination. They are then designated *certified rehabilitation counselors.*

Some states require counselors in public employment offices to have master's degrees; others accept bachelor's degrees with appropriate counseling courses.

Mental health counselors generally have master's degrees in mental health counseling, in other areas of counseling, or in psychology or social work. They are voluntarily certified by the National Board of Certified Clinical Mental Health Counselors. Generally, to receive this certification, a counselor must have a master's degree in counseling, two years of post-master's experience, a period of supervised clinical experience, a taped sample of clinical work, and a passing grade on a written examination.

Some employers provide training for newly hired counselors. Many have work-study programs so that employed counselors can earn graduate degrees. Counselors must participate in graduate studies, workshops, institutes, and personal studies to maintain their certificates and licenses.

Persons interested in counseling should have a strong interest in helping others and the ability to inspire respect, trust, and confidence. They should be able to work independently or as part of a team.

Prospects for advancement vary by counseling field. Rehabilitation, mental health, and employment counselors may become supervisors or administrators in their agencies. Some counselors move into research, consulting, or college teaching or go into private practice.

Jobs in public agencies may also require an M.S.W. Supervisory, administrative, and staff training positions usually require at least an M.S.W.

In 1994, the Council on Social Work Education accredited 383 B.S.W. programs and 117 M.S.W. programs. There were fifty-six doctoral programs for the Ph.D. in social work degree and for the D.S.W. (doctor of social work). B.S.W. programs prepare graduates for direct service positions such as caseworker or group worker positions. They include courses in social work practice, social welfare policies, human behavior and the social environment, and social research methods. Accredited B.S.W. programs require at least 400 hours of supervised field experience.

An M.S.W. degree prepares graduates to perform assessments, to manage cases, and to supervise other workers. Master's programs usually last two years and include 900 hours of supervised field instruction or internship.

Entry into an M.S.W. program does not require a bachelor's degree in social work, but courses in psychology, biology, sociology, economics, political science, history, social anthropology, urban studies, and social work are recommended. Some schools offer accelerated M.S.W. programs for those with B.S.W. degrees.

Since 1993, all states and the District of Columbia have had licensing, certification, or registration laws regarding social work practice and the use of professional titles. In addition, voluntary certification is offered by the National Association of Social Workers (NASW), which grants ACSW (Academy of Certified Social Workers) or ACBSW (Academy of Certified Baccalaureate Social Workers) certification to those who qualify.

For clinical social workers, professional credentials include listing in the NASW *Register of Clinical Social Workers* or in the *Directory of American Board of Examiners in Clinical Social Work*. These credentials are particularly important for those in private practice; some health insurance providers require them for reimbursement.

Social service professionals should be emotionally mature, objective, and sensitive to people and their problems. They must be able to handle responsibility, work independently, and maintain good working relationships with clients and coworkers.

Volunteering, internships, or paid counselor or social work aide jobs offer ways of testing one's interest in this field.

JOB OUTLOOK

Social workers and counselors held about 722,000 jobs in 1994. Nearly 40 percent of the jobs were in state, county, or municipal government agencies, primarily in human resources, social services, child welfare, mental health, health, housing, education, corrections, and public welfare, and in facilities for the mentally retarded and developmentally disabled.

Employment of social service professionals is expected to increase faster than that of most occupations through the year 2005. The number of older people, who are more likely to need social services, is growing rapidly. In addition, requirements for social workers will grow with increases in the need for and concern about services to the mentally ill, the mentally retarded, and individuals and families in crisis.

Many job openings will also arise due to the need to replace social service workers who leave the occupation.

Employment in government should grow about as fast as the average in response to increasing needs for public welfare and family services.

Employment of social service professionals in private social service agencies is projected to grow about as fast as the average. Although demand for their services is expected to increase rapidly, agencies will increasingly restructure services and hire more lower-paid human services workers instead of social workers.

Competition for jobs for social service professionals is stronger in cities where training programs for counselors and social workers abound; rural areas often find it difficult to attract and retain qualified staff.

Similar to other government jobs, employment counseling jobs, offered primarily by state and local governments, could be limited by budgetary constraints. Employment counseling jobs in private job training services, however, should grow rapidly as counselors provide skill training and other services to a growing number of laid-off workers, experienced workers seeking new or second careers, full-time homemakers seeking to enter or reenter the workforce, and workers who want to upgrade their skills.

Rehabilitation and mental health counselors should be in strong demand. Insurance companies increasingly provide for reimbursement of counselors, enabling many counselors to move from schools and government agencies to private practice.

The number of people who need rehabilitation services will rise as advances in medical technology continue to save lives that only a few years ago would have been lost.

In addition, legislation ensuring equal employment rights for persons with disabilities will spur demand for counselors. Counselors not only will help individuals with disabilities with their transition into the workforce, but also will help companies comply with the law. More rehabilitation and mental health counselors also will be needed as the elderly population grows, and as society focuses on ways of developing mental well-being, such as controlling stress associated with job and family responsibilities.

SALARIES

Social workers employed by the federal government averaged $44,000 in 1995.

Median earnings for full-time educational and vocational counselors and social workers were about $30,000 a year in 1993.

RELATED FIELDS

Through direct counseling or referral to other services, social service professionals help people solve a range of personal problems. Workers in occupations with similar duties include the clergy, counselors, clinical psychologists, student personnel workers, teachers, personnel workers and managers, human services workers, psychiatrists, occupational therapists, training and employee development specialists, and equal employment opportunity/affirmative action specialists.

INTERVIEW
Jane E. Bennett
Vocational Rehabilitation Counselor

Jane E. Bennett works for the Department of Rehabilitative Services for the Commonwealth of Virginia in Fairfax, Virginia. She earned her B.S. in 1984 in Leisure Studies and Services in Therapeutic Recreation from Old Dominion University in Norfolk, Virginia. In 1990, she earned her M.A. in human resource development and rehabilitation counseling from George Washington University in Washington, D.C.

What the Job Is Really Like

"I carry a caseload of about 130 clients. I provide case management, guidance and counseling, career exploration, training, job search assistance, job placement assistance, employer contact, and education about disabilities to employers. I am responsible for providing services to my clients based on what their needs are in order to return to the workforce. We are an eligibility program in that we follow criteria for determining a client eligible for services. The criteria are these: (1) the person must have documentation of a disability; (2) this disability must pose a barrier to employment; (3) the client needs DRS [Department of Rehabilitative Services] to go back to work; and (4) the client is stable physically and mentally to benefit from the services.

"If a client is found eligible for services, then the client and I develop what is called an *individual written rehabilitation plan*. This plan includes the steps the client must take in order to return to the workforce. Therefore, each plan is very specific to the individual and his or her needs for returning to work. Some may need services as simple as guidance and counseling; writing a resume; learning how to interview and job search. Others may need skills training that takes some time to obtain. The program is very individually based and each client is treated in that manner.

"Rehabilitation counselors can work in the public industry or private industry. Working in the public industry requires a great deal of paperwork. I feel in order to do my job I need to be a good time manager as well as a good organizer. My job is very busy. Caseloads tend to be rather large, leaving very little room for downtime on the job. I use every bit of my eight hours a day to do my job. Sometimes I do work over forty hours a week but not often because of the threat of burnout. This is a job that needs to be left at the office once your day is done.

"In a typical day, I see four to five clients for one hour apiece and complete field notes and paperwork for each of these clients. The telephone is probably the most important piece of equipment used in my job. If you don't like the telephone, do not go into rehabilitation counseling. I probably get anywhere from twenty to forty phone calls a day. If I can get the calls just as they are coming in—great. If not, the calls tend to stack up and I find myself trying to return twenty-plus phone calls at the end of the day. That keeps me very busy, but I'm the type of person who wants to stay busy in a job and I don't mind paperwork. Paperwork is one of the reasons that people leave this job.

"My caseload is about 85 percent psychiatrically impaired. I also work with physically impaired, mentally retarded, and learning disabled people. The whole focus of my job is to assist persons with disabilities in returning to the workforce after the onset of a disability or for them to obtain employment for the first time. We are not just in the business of finding people jobs, but we are in the business of helping people decide on a career and helping them to move in that direction.

"The best part of the job is seeing the clients succeed and improve on their lives and watch their self-esteem and self-worth just blossom. A lot of my clients have dealt with failures all their lives and don't feel that success can happen for them. When it does, it's amazing. It doesn't get any better than that."

How Jane E. Bennett Got Started

"Once I was employed by DRS, I was sent to a two-week training entitled *New Counselor Training*. At this training I was taught the process of rehabilitation from intake with the client to closure of the case. Not all state DRS agencies provide this, but it is a requirement for Virginia counselors and very beneficial.

"I have been through a variety of trainings as a state employee as well, including Americans with Disabilities Act training, working with the deaf and hard of hearing training; computer training; working with difficult clients training; working with head-injured clients training; and rehabilitation technology training—just to mention a few. In the three years I have been with DRS, I have attended about two to three training sessions a year.

"In my careers I have always worked with persons with disabilities, first as a recreation therapist and now as a rehabilitation counselor. When I made the change to rehabilitation counseling, I had decided that I still wanted to continue working with persons with disabilities—but in a counseling role. After quite a bit of research, I decided on rehabilitation counseling. I enjoy working with my clients and assisting them to become more independent and increasing their quality of life."

Expert Advice

"For someone wanting to go into rehabilitation counseling, I would say, if you are organized, are a good time manager, and enjoy assisting people in increasing their quality of life, then go for it.

"This is a busy yet very rewarding career. There are times when this job can get overwhelming, but those times are minimized by the success stories. Do not come into this profession looking for an easy, lazy job, because it isn't. It is a challenging career that keeps you on your toes."

● ● ●

FOR MORE INFORMATION

For information about career opportunities in social work, contact

National Association of Social Workers
750 First Street NE, Suite 700
Washington, DC 20002-4241

National Network for Social Work Managers
6501 North Federal Highway, Suite 5
Boca Raton, FL 33487

An annual directory of accredited B.S.W. and M.S.W. programs is available for $10 from

Council on Social Work Education
1600 Duke Street
Alexandria, VA 22314-3421

For general information about counseling, as well as information on specialties such as school, college, mental health, rehabilitation, multicultural, career, marriage and family, and gerontological counseling, contact

American Counseling Association
5999 Stevenson Avenue
Alexandria, VA 22304

For information on accredited counseling and related training programs, contact

Council for Accreditation of Counseling and Related Educational Programs
American Counseling Association
5999 Stevenson Avenue
Alexandria, VA 22304

For information on national certification requirements and procedures for counselors, contact

National Board for Certified Counselors
3-D Terrace Way
Greensboro, NC 27403

For information about rehabilitation counseling, contact

National Rehabilitation Counseling Association
1910 Association Drive
Reston, VA 22091

National Council on Rehabilitation Education
Department of Special Education
Utah State University
Logan, UT 84322-2870

For information on certification requirements for rehabilitation counselors, contact

> Commission on Rehabilitation Counselor Certification
> 1835 Rohlwing Road, Suite E
> Rolling Meadows, IL 60008

State employment service offices have information about job opportunities and entrance requirements for counselors.

Information on academic programs in human services may be found in most directories of two- and four-year colleges, available at libraries or career counseling centers.

For information on programs and careers in human services, contact

> National Organization for Human Service Education
> Brookdale Community College
> Lyncroft, NJ 07738

> Council for Standards in Human Service Education
> Montgomery Community College
> 340 Dekalb Pike
> Blue Bell, PA 19422

Information on job openings may be available from state employment service offices or directly from city, county, or state departments of health, mental health and mental retardation, and human resources.

About the Author

A full-time writer of career books, Blythe Camenson is mainly concerned with helping job seekers make educated choices. She firmly believes that, with enough information, readers can find long-term, satisfying careers. To that end, she researches traditional as well as unusual occupations, talking to a variety of professionals about what their jobs are really like. In all of her books she includes firsthand accounts from people who can reveal what to expect in each occupation—the upsides as well as the downsides.

Camenson's interests range from history and photography to writing novels. She is also director of Fiction Writer's Connection, a membership organization providing support to new and published writers.

Camenson was educated in Boston, earning her B.A. in English and psychology from the University of Massachusetts and her M.Ed. in counseling from Northeastern University.

In addition to *On the Job: Real People Working in Government*, she has written more than two dozen career books in a variety of professional fields.